PROFESSIONALS ON WORKPLACE STRESS

The Essential Facts Series

Bright/The EU: Understanding the Brussels Process
0-471-95608-2 252 pages

Cameron Markby Hewitt/Business Guide to Competition Law
0-471-95704-6 340 pages

Landman/Doing Business in the US
0-471-96160-4 326 pages

Forthcoming Titles
Barnett/Avoiding Unfair Dismissal Claims
0-471-96564-2 200 pages

Lewis/Professional Error: Identifying, Making and Defending
Negligence Claims
0-471-97207-X 300 pages

PROFESSIONALS ON WORKPLACE STRESS
The Essential Facts

Edited by
Alex Roney and Cary Cooper

JOHN WILEY & SONS

Chichester • New York • Weinheim • Brisbane • Singapore • Toronto

Copyright © 1997 by John Wiley & Sons Ltd,
Baffins Lane, Chichester,
West Sussex PO19 1UD, England

National   01243 779777
International   (+44) 1243 779777
e-mail (for orders and customer service enquiries): cs-books@wiley.co.uk
Visit our Home Page on http://www.wiley.co.uk
or http://www.wiley.com

Other Wiley Editorial Offices

John Wiley & Sons, Inc., 65 Third Avenue,
New York, NY 10158-0012, USA

WILEY-VCH Verlag GmbH, Pappelallee 3,
D-69469 Weinheim, Germany

Jacaranda Wiley Ltd, 33 Park Road, Milton,
Queensland 4064, Australia

John Wiley & Sons (Asia) Pte Ltd, 2 Clementi Loop #02-01,
Jin Xing Distripark, Singapore 129809

John Wiley & Sons (Canada) Ltd, 22 Worcester Road,
Rexdale, Ontario M9W 1L1, Canada

Library of Congress Cataloging-in-Publication Data
Professionals on workplace stress — the essential facts/edited by
Alex Roney and Cary Cooper.
        p.   cm.—(Essential facts series)
    Includes bibliographical references and index.
    ISBN 0-471-97651-2 (pbk.)
    1. Job stress.   2. Job stress—Great Britain.   3. Work—
    Psychological aspects.   I. Roney, Alex. II. Cooper, Cary L.
    III. Series.
    HF5548.85.P766   1997
    158.7—dc21   97-23239
                                                            CIP

British Library Cataloguing in Publication Data
A catalogue record for this book is available from the British Library

ISBN 0-471-97651-2

Typeset in 11/13pt Times by C.K.M. Typesetting, Salisbury, Wiltshire.
Printed and bound in Great Britain by Biddles Ltd, Guildford and King's Lynn.
This book is printed on acid-free paper responsibly manufactured from sustainable forestation,
for which at least two trees are planted for each one used for paper production.

CONTENTS

3. ## Human Resource Perspective on Managing Stress
   Jose Pottinger

4. ## An Occupational Physician's Experience of Workplace Stress
   David Moore

CONTRIBUTORS' PROFILES

Alex Roney

Mrs Roney was one of the first stagiaires after the United Kingdom joined the EC to go to work for the Commission in Brussels. She was the Legal Counsellor at the London Chamber of Commerce and Industry from 1973 to March 1997, dealing with a range of matters, and has now joined the market research team at Winmark Ltd.

She is the author of the EC/EU Fact Book, now in its 4th Edition and has contributed to and edited several other books, including *Appointing Commercial Agents in Europe* published in 1996 by John Wiley and also the forthcoming *Professional Error: Identifying, Making and Defending Claims.*

She is an external examiner in European law for the South Bank University, and a member of the exclusive Club of Rhodes (only for ex-nominees and recipients of the Woman of Europe award), and is on various committees.

Enthusiastic about the environment, Alex Roney is Deputy Chairman of the London in Bloom campaign committee which encourages local authorities, businesses and residents to make London a more attractive place in which to live and work.

As a working mother with a busy husband, two teenagers and a dog to look after, she has some experience of the strains imposed particularly on women.

Cary Cooper

Cary L. Cooper is currently Professor of Organizational Psychology in the Manchester School of Management, and Pro-Vice-Chancellor (External Activities) of the University of Manchester Institute of Science and Technology (UMIST). He is the author of over 70 books (on occupational stress, women at work and industrial and organisational psychology), has written over 250 scholarly articles for academic journals, and is a frequent contributor to national newspapers, TV and radio. He is currently Editor-in-Chief of the *Journal of Organizational Behavior*, co-Editor of the medical journal *Stress Medicine*, and Fellow of the British Psychological Society, The Royal Society of Arts and The Royal Society of Medicine. Professor

Cooper was also the Founding President of the British Academy of Management.

Jose Pottinger

Fellow of the IPD and currently Vice-President Pay and Employment, Jose Pottinger combines a highly experienced human resources background with an in-depth understanding of the modern business environment. Her career over more than 20 years has extended across FMCG and engineering, with many notable achievements in both line and corporate management.

Jose's skills are fully utilised in her current position as Personnel Director with Cummins Engine Company. Cummins is a leading American multinational diesel engine manufacturer; it had sales of over $5.2 billion in 1995 and employs around 24,000 people with manufacturing operations in 15 countries supported by a customer service network in some 5,000 locations throughout the world. Working on a broad international basis, Jose's demanding responsibilities range from corporate strategic planning to joint venture business development and operational support for marketing. During this time Jose has been at the forefront of introducing innovative training and personal development programmes, playing a key role in developing a highly successful quality-led culture throughout the organisation.

As an acknowledged senior professional, Jose has delivered papers at Harrogate, the European Committee for Work and Pay, the European Institute for Advanced Studies in Management and for Industrial Society seminars.

Jose's wide knowledge and experience is also reflected by her membership of the Panel for Industrial Tribunals, as visiting lecturer at Durham University Business School and as visiting lecturer and external examiner for the IPD element of the MA in Human Resources at Newcastle University Business School from which establishment she achieved her own MBA. She is also a member of the editorial advisory board of the *Human Resource Management Journal.*

David Moore

Dr David A. Moore is Director of Group Medical Services for Scottish and Newcastle plc (the United Kingdom's largest brewer, employing more than 45,000 people, principally in the United Kingdom but also in the Benelux countries, Germany, France and Ireland. He is a consultant occupational physician with a background in the Armed Services, the shipping, transport and warehousing industry and now in the brewing, retail and leisure businesses. He has been interested in stress problems since the early 1980s and began work on the subject in his company in 1986. Interested more in prevention than in therapeutic action, in 1990, and in conjunction with Professor Cooper of UMIST, his department carried out a large-scale stress audit of employees. This study identified the principal causes of, and the employee groups affected by, stress and a programme of preventative action was followed. This programme was evaluated through a further stress audit and significant evidence of improvement was demonstrated.

Elaine Aarons

Elaine Aarons Solicitor LLB (Hons) (University of London) has specialised in employment law since 1982. She is the Head of Employment Law at the London office of Eversheds where 12 solicitors specialise exclusively in this area. Eversheds is the second largest firm in the United Kingdom and Europe. Out of over 1,300 lawyers in the United Kingdom, there are 84 employment law specialists making up the largest employment law group in any United Kingdom law firm.

She is on the Management Committee of the Employment Lawyers' Association of which she is Training Co-ordinator. She is also a member of the Labour Law Sub-committee of the International Bar Association, and an active member of the City of London Solicitors' Company Employment Law Sub-Committee. She lectures and writes regularly, and has recently co-written a book on *Flexible Working Practices* for Croners. Elaine's emphasis is to advise in context, offering practical solutions; she works closely with other disciplines in the personnel field such as management consultants and human resource consultants. In 1996 Elaine was highly recommended as a specialist in her field by *Legal 500 and Chambers Directory*.

Claire Wilson

Claire Wilson was born in Northern Ireland, and went to St Andrew's University, Scotland, where she achieved an MA in English Language and English Literature.

After a varied career in business, she became editor of a trade magazine. More recently she has been working as a freelance journalist and has written for IPC, *The Observer* and a number of trade magazines, specialising in international trade.

Jonathan Cooke

Jonathan Cooke graduated from the Camberwell School of Art in 1981, and the Chelsea College of Art in 1982. Since then he has exhibited not only in the United Kingdom, but also in Japan, where he is strongly represented, although galleries in Barcelona and Athens also sell his work. He has carried out some unusual commissions, including the tapestry designs for the Momra Art Programme in Jeddah, Saudi Arabia in 1993.

As may be seen from this book, he enjoys drawing cartoons, but his work encompasses many forms of art, and he presently particularly enjoys working with marble.

FOREWORD

I am delighted to have been invited to write the Foreword to *Professionals on Workplace Stress* which includes work by some of the foremost experts in the field of stress. This book not only seeks to develop an acceptable definition of stress and how it relates to the workplace, but also gives practical advice on preventative and coping strategies.

Various sources put the cost to the United Kingdom economy of stress in the workplace at between £5 and £7 billion a year. But it is not just about money. It is also about individuals.

The TUC's 1996 survey of safety representatives identified stress as the top workplace safety concern. More than two-thirds of over 7,000 respondents to the survey (68 per cent), from across all occupational groups, identified stress as the main hazard in their workplace.

People working in the voluntary sector and in education were the most likely to highlight concerns about stress, identifying overwork and stress as the main hazard in their workplaces. In addition, stress was identified as the worst workplace health and safety problem in leisure services, local government, central government, transport and communication and other service sectors.

It also seems that the lower you are down the workplace pecking order, the worse the stress. The main problems are workload, a lack of control over how the job is done and bad management style.

Homeworking, teleworking and telecottaging are often touted as the liberating, family-friendly twenty-first century way of working. Not so. Nearly six out of ten homeworkers suffer from mental health problems, including stress and depression.

Twenty years ago, union surveys identified workplace stress as a genuine occupational health concern. Then employers and the health and safety enforcement authorities either ignored the problem or said it was "just part of the job".

Today, trade unions in the United Kingdom have developed high quality educational materials and courses and detailed guidance to members so that trade union Safety Representatives—there are 200,000 of them nationwide—can identify the causes and effects of workplace stress and can put their case for the stressors to be removed from the workplace.

Union action in the workplace and the courts has made stress an issue of concern to employers and insurers. But while some of the better employers have introduced stress audits, policies and counselling, a welter of other management changes are running counter to the goal of a stress-free workplace.

Good employers will work with trade unions to eliminate work-place stress, and will think hard about the impact of bully-boy management, redundancies, insecurity and overload on their staff.

Employers, managers, trade unions and employees should employ the excellent advice in this book to develop their own answers for preventing stress in the workplace. Only by all sections of industry working together can we curb the new workplace epidemic—stress.

JOHN MONKS
GENERAL SECRETARY, TUC
24 April 1997

ACKNOWLEDGEMENTS

My thanks go to everyone who supported me with the book and in particular to John Massa who assisted me with various materials on the subject of stress, and to Elizabeth Davison, who copy-edited the book.

ALEX RONEY

1. INTRODUCTION TO WORKPLACE STRESS

1. INTRODUCTION TO WORKPLACE STRESS

Alex Roney

"I really feel stressed". How often have you heard or felt that lately? One cannot pick up a newspaper or switch on the radio or television without some form of stress being mentioned or discussed.

When you think about it, so many stressful scenarios can be envisaged—job insecurity, redundancy, unemployment, debt, having to deal with difficult customers, clients, patients or people generally. Maybe we can also imagine ourselves as the outraged person, being aggressive, fighting for our perceived rights. Both roles are stressful for the participants.

One gets the impression that people are increasingly taking out their anger and frustration, however caused, on others—either by being more irritable (at the lowest level) or by driving fast and dangerously, exploding into road rage, drinking heavily and then becoming aggressive, or by releasing some of their tensions by bullying other people either at home or at work.

The link between home life and work is important, as few people can truly separate completely the two halves of their lives. Employers must understand the implications and symptoms of stress and its related illnesses. Employees must be able to withstand its pressures, and know what to do if they feel they are becoming affected. Those at home have to have an appreciation of the problems which can arise, and the ways in which they can help. This means that everyone should know more about stress, how to recognise it and its symptoms, how to minimise it, how to manage it successfully, how to deal with it and how to help others to deal with it, from the different perspectives of individual or employee, employer, family, friend or professional adviser. This knowledge could be vitally important for you, and your close family and friends, or even your work colleagues. It is why I have asked the expert authors of this book to help, and a victim to tell her tale. Necessarily there is some duplication in the information given, but in each chapter the problem of stress is viewed from a different perspective, and the data is therefore important to the advice presented.

What is stress?

First it is important to know in general terms what stress is, and it is defined in the book by the different professionals to reflect their different perspectives.

The Health and Safety Executive have defined stress as the reaction people have to excessive pressures and other types of demand placed on them. It generally arises when they worry that they are not able to cope. What is most interesting for the layman to know is that stress can manifest itself in behavioural ways such as poor concentration, or an increase in alcohol intake, increased obsessive smoking, and irritability; or it can have physical effects. Headaches can increase in frequency and intensity, shoulders and neck may ache. There may be skin rashes, increased heart rate, or even sweating. Resistance to infection may decrease, and there may for example be dizziness. The effects may diminish with the level of stress, but it should be realised that prolonged stress can lead to nervous breakdowns, long term psychological problems, marriage breakdowns, and physical ill-health. Professor Cary Cooper will deal with this in more detail in his chapter.

What are the causes of stress?

It is easy to see how stress can be caused or increased at work. Ever higher targets; increased pressures to perform; greater workload; lack of job certainty or even job security; unmerited, or even injudicious merited criticism, uncertainty as to what is required of the employee; constant changes in work patterns or management—the list seems endless. All these are common causes of stress in the workplace. Less well appreciated are the cumulative effects of different stress factors, and it is here that many employers or managers, often under pressure of time, do not always appreciate the importance of treating each of their employees as an individual, and recognising different needs. The same applies in families, where partners are working and frequently tired, and communication limited to "What is on the telly tonight?" Transport difficulties to and from work impose their own sometimes significant irritations, and even dangers, particularly for shiftworkers.

Both family members and workplace managers must be available to watch, listen, understand and assist individuals when for example they are under extra pressures. Managers should seek to ensure that they know when an employee is subject to stress factors, "stressors" such as marital difficulties, financial worries, dependent relatives, house moves, bereavement, or other problems outside the workplace which are adding to the "normal" load of pressures. This sort of caring management attitude is likely to defuse potential stress hazards which could cause mistakes, resulting in bad workmanship or even injury to other employees.

Jose Pottinger explains in Chapter 3 how the human resources manager will look at these aspects of work-related stress, and organisational culture and leadership.

Is the work environment important?

The whole work environment is important.

There is the psychological environment. Individuals are less likely to become stressed when surrounded by pleasant behaviour, rather than personality conflicts, with understanding and firm leadership, rather than demands perceived to be unreasonable, and a lack of interest from managers. People need to be treated as people, and not made to feel like automatons or items on a balance sheet.

There is the general physical environment. A calm, pleasant, organised ambience, however busy the workplace, is less conducive to stress than a disorganised, frenetic atmosphere, with uncontrolled hazards, noise and high temperatures, and managers who require unexpected extra work from employees at short notice, with no thought for the continuity and rhythm of normal work patterns.

Facilities which work, effective machines that do not have to have "please do not kick" labels, space for individuals, relaxing colours, good lighting, clean workplaces and thought given to the physical comfort of employees whatever they are doing minimise physical stress and are all important factors which maximise work performance.

Action which can be taken by employers, and tactics they can adopt, will vary with the differing requirements of the enterprise generally, and the needs of the employees as individuals. The ways in which required action can be identified is discussed in more detail by both Professor Cooper in Chapter 2 and Dr Moore in Chapter 4. Thus at one level a change in work patterns can help—e.g. to relieve repetitive strain injuries. At another level team building can be useful, whereby the load can be shared when colleagues are undergoing particularly busy times—although it must be said that this can cause cracks too, where people are perceived not to "pull their weight". Jose Pottinger with advice for the personnel/human resources manager makes many useful suggestions in Chapter 3.

What about general health aspects?

The physical environment and well thought-out work patterns are important for general health. Eye strain, repetitive strain and other injuries can lead to an employee having difficulties in carrying out his or her job, which can itself then cause harmful stress.

Because harmful stress often leads to behavioural or physical consequences, it can often have a "knock on" effect on other employees, either by increasing their stress load or their workload, or indeed by increasing their contact with minor illnesses such as colds contracted by a stressed employee with a lowered immunity. This means that it is doubly important for employers and managers to watch out for stressful situations, and help vulnerable employees at an early stage. An increase in staff turnover or sickness in a particular department could be a symptom of a manager or other employee not only possibly suffering from stress, but maybe causing an unacceptable work environment, and so signal that action should be taken. Dr Moore gives his valuable experience as an occupational health physician in Chapter 4.

The Health and Safety Executive, in its pamphlet on the subject, expressly suggests that stress should be treated like any other health hazard. This means that procedures should be available in every workplace to prevent the build up of stress, and then to help the individuals affected. There should be recognised disciplinary procedures to deal with, for example, racial and sexual harassment and other bullying tactics by staff or managers.

Is a feeling of security important?

In general people do not like swift or unexpected changes. They like to know where and how they stand in respect of their jobs, managers and work colleagues. They like to feel secure at work and in respect of their salaries. Much comes back to recognised good management practices to make staff feel secure. There should be clear company and individual objectives which should be made known to and understood by all employees. There should be facilities for staff to have a continuing input and to be informed about the development of the enterprise for which they work. This is because one of the recognised ways in which pressure can be unconsciously put on an employee is through the feeling of impotence he or she feels concerning the development of the job, or even of the employing enterprise. Thus employees must feel they can make an individual contribution, that this is valued, and that they can be effective, whether they are full-time, part-time or contracted employees. What happens when employees are not valued and are consistently subject to the sort of stress which undermines their self confidence is graphically explained in Chapter 6 by Claire Wilson who suffered just such treatment.

In this day and age, there is a significant trend towards employers only using short term contracts in order to keep employment costs as low as possible, and moving towards a project-based work schedule wherever possible. The "down side" of this is a breaking of continuity, lack of certainty, and removal of the feelings of responsibility and loyalty owed by employers to employees and *vice versa* (see under "Changing work patterns" later in this chapter).

Visible measures should be taken as regards health and safety, to show a general concern for the health and welfare of all employees, with sensible work practices, targets, and training where appropriate to ensure that employees do not feel overwhelmed by what is expected of them. The workforce is a valuable resource, but to work at their optimum level employees, whether full or part-timers, casual or permanent, or even self-employed or subcontractors, must be correctly managed.

Does bullying count as a source of stress?

Bullying, racial and sexual harassment have recently become more prominent among the stressful hazards to be encountered in both the work and home environments.

Bullying is not a new problem, but it does appear to be growing, and it is serious. Schools encounter it. How many of us have children who have suffered some form of bullying at school? We may even have suffered ourselves. Girls are not much better than boys—they bully too, but usually in a more subtle way using verbal and psychological weapons rather than brute force. It is a deeply disturbing modern trend that young girls are increasingly becoming involved in violent crime. The suicide rate among young people, particularly young men, is alarming, and one all too often hears on the media about children and young people who have run away from home or are absentees from school. How much of this is the result of abuse, itself due to social stressful pressures such as unemployment, how much is the result of direct pressures, and how much is due to drug-related problems and sheer lack of a feeling of right and wrong, is difficult to assess. Research is now being done in the realm of preventative medicine to seek to predict future trends and establish some remedial policies.

It is generally expected that young people grow out of this bullying phase, but do they? To what extent can these tendencies resurface later? Do small boys as men in positions of power tend to bully others in a lesser position as an unconscious antidote to restore their egos bruised by bigger boys in their youth? Does a person who is a target for bullying when young remain vulnerable? Or is it all a question of the development of each individual, his or her upbringing and character? Finally, how much depends on education, and whether a child is taught the "do as you would be done by" culture, rather than the "do as well as you can and damn the rest" viewpoint? Are adults becoming frightened of children who bully, and capitulating rather than setting the rules? Are parents despised by their children when they are seen to be "soft"? Are parents blaming society generally rather than themselves when little Johnnie is caught wielding a knife? or hitting Jane over the head? It is certainly true that parents now are more likely to accede to the wishes of their children than *vice versa*.

Bullying, sometimes physical, but more often verbal, is one of the frequently less obvious causes of stress, but is important because it is often itself the manifestation of stress in the bully, and causes great unhappiness for the victims. It has a knock on effect, frequently causing the bully yet more difficulties by making his or her home life difficult, with a domino effect on work and working colleagues. Employers can no longer turn a blind eye. They can be made vicariously—and expensively—liable for the actions of their staff. Elaine Aarons deals comprehensively in Chapter 5 with the employer's legal liabilities.

What about stress management?

The individual's needs

There is positive stress, and negative stress. In other words, some people thrive on being busy, even overburdened with work, dealing with brinkmanship in a professional or other capacity. Deadlines are a joy, with a feeling of intense satisfaction when targets are met, cases won, and days are crowded with meetings and presentations. Those individuals either sleep well, or don't need much rest. They get up full of energy, ready for the fray each day, and would be bored and possibly even depressed if nothing were going on. Some people can work for years in jobs which involve watching suffering, or dealing with accidents or their aftermath, or even dangerous situations, such as the fire service or the police, and suffer no ill effects or post traumatic stress difficulties. Others, again, are deeply affected, despite proper training. Then there are people who find that if they have to do too much, their concentration is impaired, they have feelings of panic, they make mistakes, can't sleep, have headaches or migraines, become ill or depressed to a greater or lesser degree, become irritable, drink or smoke too much, or even take drugs; and the circle of harmful stress symptoms already defined above begins, with the affected person feeling out of control in respect of his or her own life.

Often a feeling of tiredness can be caused by a bad diet, and can itself lead to this circle of inability to cope. Sometimes the drugs prescribed to deal with depression or sleeplessness themselves cause more problems. Financial worries need no elaboration, but some people have higher expectations than others, which can impose extra burdens.

It is not always easy to enable a person badly affected by harmful stress to take effective control again of his or her own life, and to resume the self confidence needed to become an effective and contented member of society again. This is particularly the case where that person does not have the extra help and advice of close friends, work colleagues or family. Where the individual is self-employed, for example, there are extra strains imposed. These, too, are explored later in this book.

Stress reduction techniques

There are various methods which individuals use to enable them both physically and mentally to cope with the strains imposed on them. Some people find that exercise which helps to keep the body fit also acts as a physical release for the tensing up effects of stress and provides a relaxation. Others find massage, aromatherapy, or relaxation or meditation exercises helpful. Others again throw themselves into their hobbies or extra-work activities such as gardening or drama groups to ensure that they have distractions from the work environment, if this is where the pressures are; or from the home environment, if their stressful situations arise there. Others go to their local pub, and provided they do not become reliant on alcohol, this has provided a friendly panacea for many. However, many of these solutions are expensive, and it is a sad myth that only those with cash suffer from stress.

Some people are lucky enough to be able to "switch off" when they come home, and they are the ones least likely to suffer from harmful stress.

Employer's needs

Employers need keen, effective, trustworthy employees who can efficiently undertake the job they are employed to do. A good, well-trained and experienced workforce is a valuable workforce, and it is important to nurture it. Often the viability of the entire enterprise is based on the ability of each employee to do his or her job effectively. Mistakes can prove costly, whether they result in defective goods, services, decisions or advice. Sometimes errors can be life-threatening.

Individuals have to learn how to manage the different pressures on them. Managers ought to be able to help them to do this and so need to be able to gauge stress levels put on employees, and to guide them in stress management. This frequently means also time management and efficiency to give the individual time to enable him or her to deal with varying workloads effectively. It may mean organising team support, to ensure that the employee can meet the employer's needs. It may mean professional counselling for staff and managers where staff are facing hard times with redundancies among the workforce looming, or even when the workload is being significantly raised. Nowadays it may even mean monitoring employees to ensure that they are not working unreasonably long hours, as in the longer term this can be unproductive and leave the employer open to legal action. Professor Cooper in Chapter 2 reports that 90 per cent of employers surveyed in one study saw long hours as a problem in terms of reduced performance and lowered morale, so perhaps attitudes are changing. The Organisation of Working Time Directive 1993 which came into effect in November 1996, and which seeks to encourage limits to working hours under the umbrella of health and safety legislation, may go some way to reducing the incidence of this, as it will lead to closer monitoring. There are a variety of actions and techniques which employers can use to minimize the causes and so reduce the incidence of harmful stress in the workplace, and these are explored more fully later in this book.

Families' needs

Families have needs. Children need parents around as much as possible, and it is important that these requirements are kept in mind by managers, who may be able to suggest, for example, that work schedules of employees as a matter of principle should avoid imposing extra stress on family relationships, difficulties which could prove to be the extra straw building towards a hazardous stress situation. Flexibility as to hours worked can lift a significant burden of strain particularly from women employees with children to think of.

The pressures nowadays, particularly on professionals to remain up to date with a vast volume of changing information and to deliver services promptly, often means that work must be done at home in the evenings and at weekends. The official hours of the working week are insufficient. This can have the dual effect of putting extra pressures on families, and turning the home environment into a work environment. An individual can thence be sucked into a situation whereby he is unable to get away from his work environment to rest. This can be a particular problem for self-employed people who work from home.

In a stress situation, where an employee is suffering from the adverse effects of stress, it may be wise to ensure that families, as well as the individual concerned, are counselled to help them all deal with the problem. Husbands and wives, partners and other family members can be of enormous help (or indeed hindrance) to an individual under heavy pressures at work. The urge to spend money, and lack of understanding about the difficulty of earning it can also contribute to extra strains being put on individuals, and expert counselling can help.

Society's needs

Society needs well-balanced citizens. It does not need people who suffer from road rage, alcoholism and drug abuse, or people who take out their frustrations in child abuse, the effects of which often continue into the next generation, besides causing untold suffering now. Society requires surgeons with steady hands, professionals with clear heads who don't add to the problems of their clients, nurses who are not so pressurised that they don't have time to read the precise prescriptions, drivers, craftsmen and construction workers who know what they are doing, patient parents and teachers, and many others. Society needs to ensure as far as possible that individuals do not get into an over-stressed state of mind, such that they are out of control in terms of their actions which could affect themselves and others. Besides humanitarian considerations, harmful stress costs society a great deal in terms of lost working time and expertise, medical care and benefits, besides the costs to the employer of recruiting and training new personnel. Professor Cooper in Chapter 2 details some surprising statistics as to costs.

Rights and duties

People have legal duties and responsibilities not only to their families and friends, but also to other people who might be affected directly by, or even as a consequence of, their actions. This applies equally to where they are acting under stress, or imposing harmful stress on others. They may have rights against an employer for example. All this is explained in more detail by Elaine Aarons in Chapter 5.

Changing work patterns and the move towards more temporary work

These are now operating as significant stressors, or causes of stress for many people. It is becoming the norm for wives or female partners to work as well as their male counterparts. Usually this is for financial reasons, to supplement the family income—to help to pay the day-to-day outgoings, for the mortgage, the children's education, holidays, or even that new three piece suite... Sometimes a woman will work to continue her career, and sometimes because the work environment has taken the place of a home "social" daytime environment.

Two further elements are important to note: the fact that women traditionally are used to doing lower-paid part-time work means that they are ready candidates for the new available short term or part-time jobs that are on offer, which are not usually geared to attract the main breadwinner of a family, who ideally will seek a more long term, better paid situation. As everyone knows who undertakes a part-time job, hours can frequently be stretched, and the volume of work expected is often more than the stipulated hours can contain. However, increasingly these may be the only jobs available, especially in areas of high unemployment, and this can cause extra strains on relationships where it is the woman who is the only worker in a family.

Secondly, with the increase in one-parent families, it is often the mother who must bear a number of cumulatively exhausting roles at home: breadwinner, housewife, mother, family disciplinarian—the list seems endless. This burden can be a significant cause of stress, and may make the person more vulnerable to difficulties at work.

Debt as a stressor

Another source of stress is the credit syndrome. People are bombarded on all sides to "buy now, pay later" and can get into dire financial positions where they can see no way out. Unpaid mortgage instalments can eventually lead to dispossession of homes.

Longer hours will not necessarily pay the bills, which can swiftly mount up if, even for a short period, a person cannot earn the usual amount—through ill-health for example. The sickness may not even be their own, but that of a family member. Help is available, however, and any manager identifying an employee in this kind of difficulty would do well to offer to arrange for, or at least to urge the employee to take the advice of a good credit counsellor.

Gambling

This is another addiction which is growing particularly among young men in this country according to surveys, and it can lead vulnerable employees swiftly into difficulties, causing desperate and sometimes criminal behaviour. Disappointment at losing may encourage a desire to forget it all, and drink or take drugs, and then even steal from fellow employees. It may lead to a deterioration in appearance as there is no money left to buy clothes. Nerves may become frayed, and irritation taken out on other employees—and the stressor at work is born. Those problems often fly, like homing pigeons, back to the desk of the (human resources) manager.

Are some people more at risk from stress than others?

Anyone can be at risk if they are subjected to the kind of stressors which affect them, but some people are more obviously at risk than others. Most people have a sensitive area, but some individuals work much better if they are managed in a particular way. Creativity and innovative ideas are vital for the successful organisation, and both are often reliant on creative people, who are widely thought of as being unusual, maybe temperamental, but always particularly sensitive to criticism. Not the best people on whom to push the pressures of today when fast results are demanded. "You want it good, or you want it Friday?" is an old joke, but anathema to the creative person whether he be artist, copy-writer, or marketing strategist. Competitive pressures are here to stay. Reasonable deadlines are acceptable and an important part of the working life of some individuals. It is the managers who will have to make seemingly impossible deadlines into exciting challenges, and protect the creators from pettifogging interruptions or bureaucratic requirements.

It is important, too, to realise that creativity can be required not just from the obvious categories, such as creative artists and actors, but also from sales teams, business development departments, teachers, and even policemen undertaking investigations. Research has shown that creative people are often self-motivated, but their lives tend to be bound up in their work. Difficult, but rewarding for the successful boss or team leader.

Are there any general rules for managers?

It seems that the way in which the best managers operate is often governed by their own experiences, the principle of "do as you would be done by", and necessity. They are probably more prone than most in the organisation to be placed in stressful situations. It is hard to make others redundant, or to discipline or dismiss someone, with whom at a personal level you might have considerable sympathy. A clear conscience does help.

It is always best to avoid problems whenever possible, and an increasingly important area is matching the person to the job. The use of specialised interviewing techniques are being used more and more to identify an applicant's strengths and weaknesses, and these can be stressful for both the interviewer and the interviewee. The person recruiting has to be careful not to contravene any provisions relating to discrimination, whether racial, sexual, or, since December 1996 in the United Kingdom on grounds of disability—and this can include previous mental illness for example.

According to Reed Personnel Services, now the United Kingdom's biggest recruitment agency, many of the first stage job interviews of the future will be held using video conferencing techniques, and different presentational skills will be needed, both for the interviewer and successful job applicant. Even before the job advertisement goes out, the employer should think carefully about and discuss require-ments with the line manager and others affected by the appointment. Often the perfect candidate is hidden among existing employees, but the temptation to promote someone above their capabilities should be avoided. All too often the successful applicant does not really know about the challenges he or she will face if the job is accepted, and if expectations are too high, or capabilities too low, difficulties can result. All this means more responsibility is imposed on the recruiting manager.

Another area where a good manager can make all the difference is where employees are put under great pressures to achieve good results, possibly in terms of high returns on investments, or high sales figures, or the achieving of other difficult targets where the employee may be tempted to take unacceptable risks, or even falsify figures, when in normal circumstances the same employee would be a perfectly honest, hardworking member of staff. A single false report can escalate into a significant difficulty. The effects of insufficiently close monitoring of a single employee put under these pressures has been graphically illustrated, for example, by the relatively recent predicament of Barings Bank.

The way in which managers should work is explored in more detail by Jose Pottinger in Chapter 3.

Stress and the self-employed

The particular strains put on people, often when they have already passed through the tunnel of redundancy, is examined in more detail in Chapter 6 through the personal experiences of Claire Wilson, but it may be useful to put in here a few reminders about how to avoid more stress than is necessary.

If you are one of those moving into self-employment for the first time, then you must first think carefully about what you, as an individual, have to offer—experience, information, particular skills or whatever. You must then look at and research the particular market for your goods or services. How big is it? Is it viable? How strong is the competition? It is vital to research this *before* you set up. So many small businesses go under (and the proprietor's redundancy cushion is spent) because this has not been done thoroughly.

The next step is to find out about and take what training and help is on offer, even if you think you don't need it. You will undoubtedly learn something, and you will have a chance to network with others on the course, and swap experiences. It may help, too, with your self confidence which, if you have just left another career, may be at a low ebb.

Before you even look for work, you would be wise to set up an efficient records system, and effective invoicing and late payment recovery systems. A very useful tool to help you to do this is the 1996 British Standard B57890 Method for Achieving Good Payment Performance in Commercial Transactions, which not only gives guidance, but if formally complied with, may help to achieve better credit terms with suppliers. You must also have smart stationery with full details of your address, telephone and preferably fax numbers in large letters so that they will not be obscured in fuzzy faxes. You would be wise to have an answerphone or telephone-answering service. There is nothing more off-putting than being unable to contact someone swiftly. "Not there? Try someone else". You can imagine the scenario.

Lastly, look and be as efficient as possible in what you do, and how you do it, but ensure that you are fully covered by insurance for any mistakes, or for difficulties arising should you become ill, or otherwise be unable to work for a while and so carry out your contracts. Make sure that you have found professional advisers whom you can approach quickly should this be necessary, and don't just rely on your bank manager, who is not there just to help you, but also to increase and protect the profits of the bank. Stressful pressures will undoubtedly be there to plague you, but you can at least minimize your day-to-day problems.

General observations

It can be seen from this introduction that stress is no respecter of persons. It can affect anyone, irrespective of the kind of profession or work they are concerned with. It is also a growing problem, as the speed of communications and pressures of modern life increase the depth of awareness of everyone. Normal life is not always easy. There are inevitably bereavements and illnesses, rows and household dramas of one sort or another.

Sitting at home listening to the radio or spending our leisure time watching TV, we are all forced to experience and understand the terrible stresses and strains of other people who are suffering from the effects of war, famine, the death or even murder of their children and so many other horrors which we read about and see on the media whether fact or fiction. People are constantly encouraged to seek financial and other success, rather than to be contented with what they have, and at the same time encounter the difficulties of living in a country with 2 million people unemployed, who have little hope of achieving those goals. One finds people putting pressure on children as young as four years old to pass tests or exams, with parents grumbling about the stress put on *them* by their children's exams. Any failure is felt—and often attributable to the fault of something—bad teachers, dyslexia, or particular learning difficulties. It is not just accepted as a part of life. These attitudes must start a very slippery slope to success. It is hardly surprising that some people reach their stress thresholds at an early age.

As an ordinary observer of human nature, as a wife, mother, employee, professional adviser, and writer, I am greatly concerned at the apparent increase in the incidence of symptoms of harmful stress in our modern society, and in seeking to get this book written, I have had to think more about this sad but fascinating subject. It now seems to me, taking what may be regarded as a simplistic view, that pressure levels are greatly contributed to by the suppressing of what I call "the good neighbour" moral or principle, whereby people really care for each person who comes within their ambit, as an individual and not as a number, or statistic, or a human resource, or as a figure in the balance sheet.

What are the causes of the change towards this less caring environment? Are a need to achieve profits or even survival, and often a distance between those dealing with policy and those carrying it out, new elements in the work environment? Or is it just that more people are available so individuals become less valuable? Various social changes certainly contribute—such as the dispersal of the extended family, with the bonds of mutual help that it created, a shifting population, and the fact that people no longer need to live near where they work—but often travel for an hour or more to get there. This in turn means that the work colleague one likes best probably lives two hours away, and has a totally separate group of "home" friends and activities. The result is simple to see. It is difficult to socialise except close to the work environment, and this is not possible or desirable where there are families to go home to, or extra dangers in travelling at night, particularly for women. Two separate lives—a work existence, and a home existence—are the result. This may suit some people very well, but may result in others being very lonely, particularly if for some reason they lose their job.

In the past, there was a strong churchgoing tradition which applies also to non-Christian forms of worship. This is now diminishing, but it had its advantages, besides the teaching of right and wrong, for the people who attended would become local acquaintances and often friends. There were people who knew of every individual's existence, who would probably notice if he or she did not turn up for a week or two, and would be more likely to check to see if all was well if there were no family. Many activities would be organised which provided a useful social existence and interests outside the work environment, and enabled young people and old to meet others in a neutral environment. Troubles could be shared. This sharing of good times and bad is an element of secure family life, and is undoubtedly diminishing with the increase in single parent families, where one adult may be unable to share the load with small children, and children have more difficulties as they grow up in a less stable family environment.

Of course there are plenty of other activities which people can participate in, such as evening classes or drama groups, but they have to make an effort to do them, rather than it be a matter of course that they attend; and frequently a person in a stress situation has already lost a lot of the self confidence needed to undertake anything new.

Small individual flats, the loss of the village ethic, and a constantly mobile population are definite factors in loneliness. It is not easy for new graduates, for example, moving from a home or student environment full of friends to find a social life in a large city where they are very small fry. The TV and videos which can so often be a substitute for going out or seeing friends must also take their part of the blame in leading to loneliness, which I would arrow as an important factor contributing to the level of stress, and which can feed on itself in some cases, particularly when an individual has nothing else to think about but his or her problems.

It is well known that racial, cultural and religious differences can cause stressful difficulties to erupt. These are often caused by basic misconceptions about culture, or the lack of it, about mores and attitudes. I once had a Muslim au pair who was very surprised to see our quiet family lifestyle. She had been conditioned to think that non-Muslim westerners were amoral, and was initially quite frightened at the prospect of living in our society. An extreme example perhaps, but it does illustrate that where multi-cultural staff are employed in an enterprise, a lot of problems might be avoided if all staff could be encouraged to learn about the different religions, origins, cultures and more of their work colleagues.

Constantly travelling or overworked parents who have to put in long hours, have already been mentioned. These sorts of jobs put particular strains on women, who by reason of their gender and probably lower pay, are usually expected to take over when children are ill or normal arrangements fail. I approve of working wives and mothers where this suits the individual (of course, I am one myself) but I do think it can be a hard life, and that the situation of an exhausted person in the house with a heavy load of responsibility at home and at work, and probably riddled with feelings of guilt about not always being there to care for children, does bring its own problems. So can boredom and a feeling of inadequacy. Nevertheless it is certainly the case that many more women now expect not only to work, but also to pursue careers in a meaningful way, partly for financial reasons, partly for their own fulfilment, and partly because unconsciously perhaps, they recognise that it is statistically the case that they may one day find themselves to be single or single parents. However working partners do create a different home environment to that encountered some years ago, and may result in men taking on additional burdens of assisting in the home. Not a bad thing, perhaps, but it does mean they can't necessarily just relax when they come home.

So many factors, so many causes and so many cases.

Is there any general advice for a person who is beginning to feel the effects of harmful stress?

Supposing you are that person, what can you do yourself if you feel you are suffering or are beginning to suffer from harmful stress?

You should take a long hard look at your life. Check out your health—because if you are suffering from more infections than usual, they may well be caused by stress (perhaps combined with tiredness in a "vicious circle" because of extra workloads after absences).

You should make sure that you are not too sorry for yourself; that you are not over-dramatising a situation; that you judge yourself and others involved honestly, but not too critically; that you make sure that you have interests outside your work environment, which should not be the only centre of your existence. Make sure you are not becoming too self-centred, self-absorbed or selfish.

You should eat sensibly and try to find time to do some form of exercise, preferable with other people—for example at a gym/badminton/football/rugby/tennis or golf club.

Ideally you should try to help others worse off than yourself (yes, there *is* always someone) because by doing so you will be doing something useful, and gaining more than you realise in confidence, and understanding, and probably friends. It is never difficult to find voluntary work, and money, although important, is not the only necessity of life. People need to feel useful. Not only you, everyone, and each person has something to give, even if it is only to make someone else feel better about their own situation.

If it is at all possible, try to make some space for yourself in the day, even if it is only five minutes. Above all, hang on to your self confidence. So many bullies and bad managers try to take control by undermining the confidence of others and making them feel inadequate. Don't let them succeed. Try to take some control over your life yourself. Always remember your good qualities and abilities. Keep hold of the truth.

All of this is easy advice to give, and maybe not so easy to follow, but it really could help you to manage the stress you are under if you can act on it in one way or another.

The purpose of this book

Of course modern life and work brings its own hardships, but this is not a gloomy book. The important thing is to be able to understand and so not only cope with stress, but also put stress to work for you, and not against you—to see life as a manageable challenge and so to achieve success with stress. However you are affected by stress, personally or through your work or home environment, whether as a manager, or work colleague, or friend or family of someone suffering, or the person suffering, it is important to know that you are not alone, and may have to learn to think positively, with considerable determination. This book is intended to help you to do just that by tapping into the expertise of its contributors. I expect that Jonathan Cooke's cartoons will make you smile a little at the everyday situations many of us have encountered.

To be affected by harmful stress is not something to be ashamed of, but it is something to be overcome. It must be used as a stepping stone experience to make the individuals concerned stronger, not weaker than before; to be more, not less sympathetic about other people's problems, and possibly to find a new purpose for their own lives.

2. IDENTIFYING SOURCES OF WORKPLACE STRESS AND A STRATEGY TO DEAL WITH THEM

2. IDENTIFYING SOURCES OF WORKPLACE STRESS AND A STRATEGY TO DEAL WITH THEM

Cary Cooper

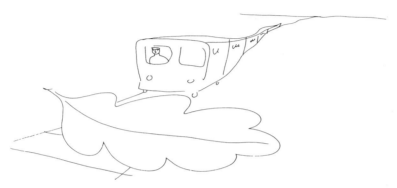

"We regret the late departure of the . . . . ."

Introduction

Every decade this century has brought its own unique changes to our working environment. In the 1960s, Harold Wilson talked about the "white heat of technology" transforming our lives, producing the 20-hour week. New technology was going to be responsible for a "leisure age" allowing us to pursue our dreams even midweek.

But instead, the 1970s brought unrest and conflict, a workplace not knowing what it was going to produce or how it was going to do it. Studs Terkel's book *Working* summed it up: "Work is by its very nature about violence—to the spirit as well as to the body. It is about ulcers as well as accidents, about shouting matches as well as fistfights, about nervous breakdowns as well as kicking the dog around. It is above all about daily humiliations. To survive the day is triumph enough for the walking wounded among the great many of us".

Then came the 1980s—the "enterprise culture"—with people working longer and harder to achieve individual success and material rewards. We had privatisation, process re-engineering (Americanised term for re-organisation), mergers and acquisitions, strategic alliances, joint ventures and the like, transforming workplaces into hothouse, free market environments. In the short term, this approach improved our economic competitiveness in international markets—but the strains started to show. "Stress" joined "junk bonds", "software packages" and "downsizing" in the modern business vocabulary—and its cost in the workplace mounted (Cooper, 1996).

The cost of stress

For United Kingdom companies in the 1980s, stress in the workplace was ten times more costly than all industrial relations disputes. In addition, the Confederation of British Industry in 1995 calculated that alcohol and drink-related diseases cost the United Kingdom economy approximately £1.7 billion annually and 8 million lost working days, with coronary artery disease and strokes costing a further 62 million days lost and mental ill-health at £3.7 billion and 91 million days lost.

The British Heart Foundation has estimated that heart disease costs the average United Kingdom company of 10,000 employees 73,000 lost working days per year, the death of 42 of its employees (between 35–64 years old) and lost productivity value to its products or services of over £2.5 million annually.

The costs of stress on the National Health Service is also currently extremely high. For example, the British Heart Foundation Coronary Prevention Group have calculated that 180,000 people die in the United Kingdom each year from coronary heart disease, that is, 500 people a day. In addition, MIND estimates that between 30 and 40 per cent of all sickness absence from work is attributable to mental and emotional disturbance. The country has also suffered from increased rates of suicide amongst the young, increasing by 30 per cent from the late 1970s to the early 1990s, particularly in the younger age groups of employees. The instability and life stress have also led to divorce rates rising from 27,000 in 1961 to 155,000 divorces by 1988, and this upward trend continues. Indeed, Relate estimates that by the year 2000 there will be four divorces in every ten marriages. And finally, Alcohol Concern estimates that one in four men in the United Kingdom drink more than the medically recommended number of units per week with 25 per cent of accidents at work involving intoxicated workers. So not only is society in general suffering from stress, but also UK plc.

Corporate cost

Why is it that many countries (e.g. USA, Finland) seem to showing declines in their levels of stress-related illnesses such as heart disease and alcoholism, while the United Kingdom's are still rising? Is it the case, for example, that American employers are becoming more altruistic and caring for their employees, and less concerned about "the bottom line"? Unfortunately the answer is a definite "no". Two trends in the USA are forcing American firms to take action. First, American industry is facing an enormous and ever spiralling bill for employee healthcare costs. Individual insurance costs rose by 50 per cent over the past two decades, but the employers' contribution rose by over 140 per cent. It has also been estimated that over $700 million a year is spent by American employers to replace the 200,000 men aged 45 to 65 who die or are incapacitated by coronary artery disease alone. Top management at Xerox estimated nearly 10 years ago that the cost of losing just one executive to a stress-related illness costs the organisation $600,000. In the United Kingdom however, employers can create intolerable levels of stress on their employees, and it is the taxpayer who picks up the bill, through the National Health Service. There is no direct accountability or incentive for firms to maintain the health of their employees. Of course, the indirect costs are enormous, but rarely does the firm actually attempt to estimate this cost: they treat absenteeism, labour turnover and even low productivity as an intrinsic part of running a business.

Secondly, there is another source of growing costs. More and more employees, in American companies at least, are litigating against their employers, through the worker compensation regulations and laws, in respect of job-related stress, or what is being termed "cumulative trauma". In the United Kingdom, we are just beginning to see a similar move toward litigation by workers about their conditions of work. Several unions are supporting cases by individual workers, and the trend is certainly in the direction of future mental disability claims, and damages being awarded on the basis of workplace stress.

Earnshaw and Cooper (1996) have highlighted many of the issues surrounding employer's liability for stress at work claims. Although employers have always been under a "duty of care" obligation in law for the health and safety of their employees, the recent case of John Walker has reinforced this (also highlighted by Elaine Aarons in Chapter 5). John Walker worked for Northumberland County Council for 17 years as a senior social work manager. He handled a large number of childcare and abuse cases, and his workload increased enormously. The population increase in the area also contributed to substantial work overload.

During 1986 the workload continued to increase and in November 1986 Mr Walker suffered a nervous breakdown. In March 1987 Mr Walker returned to work having negotiated for assistance to be provided for him on his return. As things turned out support was provided to Mr Walker on only an intermittent basis, and was withdrawn by early April. During his absence a substantial backlog of paperwork had built up which took Mr Walker till May to clear. In the meantime the number of pending cases continued to increase and Mr Walker began to experience stress symptoms once again. By September of 1987 he was advised to go on sick leave and diagnosed as being affected by a state of stress-related anxiety. In the event he suffered a second mental breakdown and was obliged to retire from his post for reasons of ill-health. The judge held that the Council were liable for Mr Walker's second nervous breakdown but not his first.

This landmark case established that foreseeable sources of workplace stress could be a health and safety issue, and employers, therefore, have a duty of care in their management of this risk. The awards for personal injury in these kinds of cases can be substantial and are forcing employers to consider strategies for the management of stress at work.

Sources of workplace stress in the 1970s and 1980s

As we have discussed, stress at work is primarily caused by the fundamentals of change, uncertainty, lack of control and high workload; all of which have become characteristic of work today. In addition, events which may be occurring in the personal domain (e.g. family or financial problems) can cause stress which often spills over into work. Because stress is cumulative, it can be quite difficult to separate cause and effect. A great deal of research has now been carried out to help identify in broad terms the sources of job and organisational stress in the workplace. The main sources of stress at work can be conceptualised as falling into six main categories: factors intrinsic to the job; the employee's role in the organisation; relationships at work; career development: organisational structure and culture; and the home/work interface.

Factors intrinsic to the job

There are a variety of factors intrinsic to the job which are potentially stressful and have been linked to poor physical and mental health. These include poor working conditions, shift work, long hours, travel, risk and danger, person-job mismatch, new technology, work overload or underload, both of a qualitative and quantative nature (Cooper and Smith, 1985; Edwards and Cooper, 1990).

The quality of the physical working environment is recognised as an important factor in employee health. In 1983, the World Health Organisation defined the concept of the "sick building syndrome". "Sick building syndrome" is characterised by a range of physiological symptoms including sensory irritation (e.g. noise, visual distractions), headache, nausea, dizziness and fatigue. Characteristically these symptoms grow worse over the course of a day and disappear after the workers leave the building. Research has found that the concentrating of macromolecular organic dust from floor coverings, the number of workplaces in an office, the age of the building, type of ventilation and other indoor climatic conditions are to be associated with the occurrence of the syndrome (Skov, Valbjorn and Pedersen, 1990).

The introduction of new technology (i.e. VDUs and word processors) may exacerbate the problem of poor ventilation (Kahn and Cooper, 1986). However, work-related ear and nasal irritation has been found to be associated with psychosocial and job-related factors such as dissatisfaction with one's supervisor and work overload (Skov, Valbjorn and Pedersen, 1990). The same study also found that office workers who considered their work pace too fast, and felt that they had little influence over their work activities, were significantly more likely to report general health symptoms. Again these factors, have been shown to be specific sources of stress amongst computer operators (Kahn and Cooper, 1986).

Numerous occupational studies have found that shift work is a common occupational stressor. As well as affecting neurophysiological rhythms such as blood temperature, metabolic rate and blood sugar levels, it has a negative impact on mental efficiency and work motivation, which ultimately result in stress-related disease (Wallace *et al*, 1988). In a study carried out among British police officers (Cooper, Davidson and Robinson, 1982), it was found that workload was a major stressor among the lower ranks, particularly police sergeants.

Eliminating or reducing stressors relating to factors intrinsic to the job may involve ergonomic solutions and have implications for task or workplace design. Problems of work overload or underload may indicate a need to recruit, skills deficiencies, under utilization or inappropriate selection decisions or delegation problems.

It must also be remembered that for many jobs like the emergency services (e.g. police, ambulance, fire service) there are a range of possible incidences which can create the conditions leading to a traumatic event. Post-traumatic stress incidents are increasingly more common as we develop more sophisticated but vulnerable technology, where people are meeting in larger numbers (e.g. rock concerts and the like) and where the pressures of society reflect themselves in increasingly aggressive behaviour (e.g. violence at work or in the home). Post-traumatic stress disorder is with us in the workplace and must be planned for and managed when it arises. Some occupations and some organisations are more "at risk" than others, but no organisation is immune, given the times we live in.

Role in the organisation

Three critical factors, role ambiguity, role conflict and the degree of responsibility for others are major sources of potential stress. In a study of American dentists (Cooper, Mallinger and Kahn, 1978), a high level of role conflict was found to be a major predictor of abnormally high blood pressure. Essentially, this conflict stemmed from the idealised "caring/healing" role and the actuality of being "an inflictor of pain". Baglioni, Cooper and Hingley (1990) identified potential role conflict amongst nurse managers between the goals of patient care and the goals of the nurse manager position. Eliminating or reducing role-related stress requires clear role definition and role negotiation.

Relationships at work

Relationships with others at work (i.e. superiors, colleagues, subordinates and customers) are potentially stressful. Strong support from peers has been found to relieve job strain, whereas mistrust of co-workers is associated with high role ambiguity, poor communication, low job satisfaction and poor psychological well-being (French and Caplan, 1970).

Improving personal relationships in the workplace is a complex process and may have implications for a range of interpersonal skills training. It may also have implications for workplace design, managerial style or organisational culture (Cooper and Williams, 1994).

Career development

Job insecurity and career development increasingly became a source of stress during the merger and acquisition boom of the 1980s and seem likely to continue so long as corporate restructuring remains a feature of the 1990s (Cartwright and Cooper, 1992). Ivancevich and Matteson (1980) have demonstrated that "career stress" is associated with multiple negative outcomes (e.g. job dissatisfaction, poor work performance, etc.). More recently Davidson and Cooper (1992) in a study of almost 1,000 United Kingdom managers, found career development blockages to be a significant stressor amongst women managers.

The introduction of regular appraisals, fairer promotion policies, the provision of retraining opportunities, career sabbaticals and counselling are ways in which career stress may be reduced. As downsizing and job loss looks set to remain a feature of organisational life in the near future, the provision of outplacement facilities becomes increasingly important.

Organisational structure and climate

Sources of stress which may be described as relating to the organisational structure and climate are frequently the outcome of organisational culture and management style. They include such factors as "office politics", lack of participation and effective consultation, restrictions on behaviour and poor communication. As the ownership and structure of so many organisations has changed during the 1980s, this has frequently resulted in culture change or collisions which serve to create ambiguous working environments and individual cultural incongruence, which are likely to be experienced as stressful. In a recent study comparing employee stress between four autonomous divisions of the same parent company, it was found that employee differences in job satisfaction, physical and mental health were linked to the culture and practices of the operating division (Cartwright, Cooper and Barron, 1993). Furthermore, such factors were also associated with motor fleet accident rates. Reducing or eliminating

stress emanating from organisational structure and climate has implications for a range of possible organisational initiatives, particularly
in the area of improved communication and policy-making.

Home/work interface

Finally, another danger of the current economic situation is the
effect that work pressures (such as fear of job loss, blocked ambition,
work overload and so on) have on home life. Managing the interface
between work and home is a potential source of stress, particularly for
dual career couples (Cooper and Lewis, 1993), or those who may be
experiencing financial difficulties or life-crises. Under normal circumstances "home" is often a refuge from the competitive and demanding
environment of work but there are circumstances when family tensions or the spillover of work-related anxieties into the home turn
domestic life into a "war zone" rather than "sanctuary".

Whilst the employing organisation can arguably do little to alleviate the stress caused by domestic circumstances such as bereavement, physical illness or marital problems other than by providing
counselling services, it can help to reduce the pressure on dual career
couples, female employees, etc., by introducing more flexible working
arrangements, career break schemes, and adopting "family friendly"
employment policies (Cooper and Lewis, 1995).

So what have the 1990s brought us, and where is the workplace of
the future heading? The early years of the decade were dominated by
the effects of the recession and efforts to get out of it. Organisations
"downsized", "delayered", "flattened", "rightsized", or whatever
euphemism one cared to use to massage the hard reality of job
losses. There are fewer people at work doing more and feeling
extremely job insecure. New technology, rather than being a saviour,
has added the burden of information overload as well as accelerating
the pace of work as a greater speed of response (for example, faxes, e-
mail, etc.) become the standard business expectation. In addition, job
insecurity is creating a climate of *presenteeism*, as individuals vie to
demonstrate "organisational commitment" in an effort to avoid the
second or third tranch of redundancies. Many work organisations are
creating "workaholic cultures", where hours of work equate in
employees' minds to productivity and even in some curious but
unproven way to efficiency.

A recent survey by Austin Knight of a million white-collar workers from 22 large United Kingdom organisations found that although three-quarters of employees sampled had contracted hours of between 35 and 37 hours a week, two-thirds regularly worked more than 40 hours, and a quarter more than 50 hours a week. 76 per cent said that continually working long hours had adversely affected their physical health and 47 per cent admitted their families suffered from their absence. Yet less than a third would "stand up to their boss to improve their family time". Ironically, 90 per cent of employers surveyed see long hours as a problem in terms of reduced performance and lowered morale.

The Institute of Management in its recent United Kingdom survey *Survival of the Fittest*, found that 81 per cent of 1,300 middle to senior managers "often or always" work longer than their official hours. 55 per cent "always" work extra hours; 54 per cent "often or always" work in the evenings and 36 per cent "often or always" work at weekends. The IM concludes that "longer working hours do not necessarily result in enhanced productivity. Excessive hours may reduce an individual's efficiency and effectiveness and consequently have a negative impact on the organisation". This was backed by the independent think tank *Demos* whose 1995 report, *Time Squeeze*, found that 25 per cent of British male employees work more than 48 hours a week; a fifth of all manual workers work more than 50 hours; one in eight managers work more than 60-hour weeks; and seven out of ten British workers want to work a 40-hour week, but only three out of ten do.

There is a price to pay—and it is paid at home; personal relations are wrecked by our culture of long working days. The BT Forum's report on the *Cost of Communication Breakdown* shows that by 1991 the United Kingdom had the highest divorce rate in Europe with 171,000 divorces per annum. Between 1961 and 1991 the proportion of people living in one-parent families increased four-fold and by 2000 the United Kingdom will have three million children and young people growing up in step-families. The fact that nearly two out of three couples are working as two earner couples makes long working hours an important social as well as organisational issue. But do the long working hours and job insecurity cultures fully explain the so-called "feel bad" factor at a time when the United Kingdom has, in contrast to many of its European competitors, positive economic indicators? Or is something more insidious going on?

The recent IM report may provide some answers. Although most United Kingdom managers found their work stressful, the hours long and the demands of their jobs on their personal relationships intrusive, their overriding anxiety concerned the future nature of work. While 72 per cent of managers perceive themselves to be "core employees", a large minority consider themselves to be on a "short term contract", or part-timers, or selling their services to organisations. In addition, more than 40 per cent of them "do not feel in control of their future career development". These constitute 58 per cent of middle managers—the next generation of senior executives. Only 25 per cent of managers "expect their next move to be a promotion within their existing organisation" while nearly 30 per cent see their future elsewhere. One in four "thought it likely they would be responsible for a dispersed work force supported by IT by the year 2000". In other words, they felt there would be a move toward the "virtual organisation".

The nature of our work environments therefore seems to be changing dramatically. Ever more organisations are implementing the dreaded words "outsourcing", "market testing", "interim management" and the like, which effectively means many more of us will be selling our services to organisations on a freelance or short term contract basis—blue collar, white collar, managerial, and professional temps. And this trend is growing faster in the United Kingdom than in any other industrialised country, particularly because the natural extension of privatising the public sector is privatising the private sector. More than one in eight British workers is self-employed, and part-time working and short term contracts are growing faster than permanent full-time work. The number of men in part-time jobs has nearly doubled in the past decade, while fewer women (under 4.5 per cent) and more men (nearly 10.5 per cent) are unemployed. Not only is the United Kingdom moving out of manufacturing industries, but also the number of people employed by firms of more than 500 employees has slumped to just over a third of the employed population.

The trend towards a "contract or freelance culture" is likely to have several consequences. More people will work from home as sophisticated IT helps to create and support the "virtual organisation". With two out of three families "two earner" or dual career, the problem of who plays what role in the family and the conflicts surrounding work and domestic peace will upset an already delicate work/home balance. If employers increasingly look for and recruit flexible workers, the likelihood is that more women will be employed, displacing men as the main breadwinner. Woman have often throughout their careers worked part-time or on short term contracts, whereas men have not. For example in 1984 there were more than four million women in part-time work, but only 570,000 men. By 1994 there were five million women and 990,000 men in part-time work. In order for women to pursue families as well as careers/jobs, a lot more women than men have had discontinuous careers.

Finally, those likely to survive the "new millennium" or "virtual organisation" will need some of the following skills; to be able to diagnose their abilities, know where to get appropriate training in deficient skills, be able to market themselves to organisations professionally, know how to network, have well developed interpersonal skills, tolerate ambiguity and a certain level of insecurity, and be able to manage time efficiently and prioritise work and family issues. Will this trend toward stable insecurity, freelance working and virtual organisational life continue? Individuals may question their need to commit themselves to organisations that are not committed to them.

Converting the "feel bad" to "feel good" factor is not simply a matter of higher salaries or greater personal rewards or a penny off income tax. Rather it involves quality of life issues, like workloads, hours of work, family time, control over one's career and some sense of job security. It is important for the future of an effective and less stressful work environment that organisations begin to think about their structures, policies and working practices with regard to their employees (Cooper, 1996).

Stress prevention and management

Any organisation which seeks to establish and maintain the best state of mental, physical and social well-being of its employees, needs to have policies and procedures which comprehensively address health and safety. These policies should include a mental health policy with procedures to manage stress based on the needs of the organisation and its employees. These should also be regularly reviewed and evaluated.

There are a number of options to consider in looking at the prevention of stress, which can be termed as **primary**, **secondary** and **tertiary** levels of prevention, and address different stages in the stress process (as described by Cooper and Cartwright (1996) in their guide to employers, *Mental Health and Stress in the Workplace*).

Primary prevention is concerned with taking action to reduce or eliminate the sources of stress and positively promoting a supportive and healthy work environment. **Secondary prevention** is concerned with the prompt detection and management of depression. **Tertiary prevention** is concerned with the rehabilitation and recovery process of those individuals who have suffered or are suffering from serious ill-health as a result of stress. To develop an effective and comprehensive organisational policy on stress, employers need to integrate these three approaches.

Primary prevention

First, the most effective way of tackling stress is to eliminate it at source. This may involve changes in personnel policies, improving communication systems, redesigning jobs, or allowing more decision-making and autonomy at lower levels. Obviously, as the type of action required by an organisation will vary according to the kinds of stressors operating, any intervention needs to be guided by some prior diagnosis or **stress audit** to identify what these stressors are and who they are affecting.

Stress audits

These typically take the form of a self-report questionnaire administered to employees on an organisational-wide, site or departmental basis. In addition to identifying the sources of stress at work and those individuals most vulnerable to stress, the questionnaire will usually measure levels of employee job satisfaction, coping behaviour, and physical and psychological health comparative to similar occupational groups and industries. Stress audits are an extremely effective way of directing organisational resources into areas where they are most needed. Audits also provide a means of regularly monitoring stress levels and employee health over time, and provide a baseline whereby subsequent intervals can be evaluated.

Diagnostic instruments, such as the Occupational Stress Indicator (Cooper, Sloan and Williams, 1988), which assesses the sources of organisational stress and health outcomes, are increasingly being used by organisations for this purpose. They are usually administered through occupational health and/or personnel/human resource departments in consultation with a psychologist. In smaller companies, there may be the opportunity to hold employee discussion groups or develop checklists which can be administered on a more informal basis. The agenda for such discussions/checklists should address the following issues:

- job content and work scheduling,

- physical working conditions,

- employment terms and expectations of different employee groups within the organisation,

- relationships at work, and

- communication systems and reporting arrangements.

Another alternative is to ask employees to keep a stress diary for a few weeks in which they record any stressful events they encounter during the course of the day. Pooling this information on a group/departmental basis can be useful in identifying universal and persistent sources of stress.

Creating healthy and supportive networks/environments
Another key factor in primary prevention is the development of the kind of supportive organisational climate in which stress is recognised as a feature of modern industrial life and not interpreted as a sign of weakness or incompetence. Mental ill-health is indiscriminate—it can affect anyone irrespective of their age, social status or job function. Therefore, employees should not feel awkward about admitting to any difficulties they encounter.

Organisations need to take explicit steps to remove the stigma often attached to those with emotional problems and maximize the support available to staff. Some of the formal ways in which this can be done include:

- informing employees of existing sources of support and advice within the organisation, like the Occupational Health Department;

- specifically incorporating self-development issues within appraisal systems;

- extending and improving the "people" skills of managers and supervisors so they convey a supportive attitude and can more comfortably handle employee problems.

Most importantly, there has to be *demonstrable commitment to the issue of stress and mental health at work* from both senior management and unions. This may require a move to more open communication and the dismantling of cultural norms within the organisation which inherently promote stress amongst employees, e.g. cultural norms which encourage employees to work excessively long hours and feel guilty about leaving "on time". Organisations with a supportive organisational climate will also be proactive in anticipating additional or new stressors which may be introduced as a result of proposed changes, e.g. restructuring or new technology, and take steps to address this, perhaps by training initiatives or greater employee involvement. Regular communication and increased employee involvement and participation play key roles in reducing stress in the context of organisational change.

Secondary prevention

Initiatives which fall into this category are generally focused on training and education, and involve awareness activities and skills training programmes.

Stress education and stress management courses

These serve a useful function in helping individuals to recognise the symptoms of stress in themselves and others and to extend and develop their coping skills and abilities and stress resilience.

The form and content of this kind of training can vary immensely but often includes simple relationship techniques, lifestyle advice and planning, basic training in time management, assertiveness and problem-solving skills. The aim of these programmes is to help employees to review the psychological effects of stress and to develop a personal stress control plan. This kind of programme can be beneficial to all levels of staff and is particularly useful in training managers to recognise stress in their subordinates and be aware of their own managerial style and its impact on those they manage. This can be of great benefit if carried out following a stress audit.

Health screening/health enhancement programmes

Organisations, with the co-operation of occupational health personnel, can also introduce initiatives which directly promote positive behaviour patterns in the workplace. Again health promotion activities can take a variety of forms. They may include:

- the introduction of regular medical checks and health screening;

- the design of "healthy" canteen menus;

- the provision of on-site fitness facilities and exercise classes;

- corporate membership with concessionary rates at local health and fitness clubs;

- the introduction of cardio-vascular fitness programmes;

- advice on alcohol and dietary control (particularly cutting down on cholesterol, salt, and sugar);

- smoking cessation programmes;

- more generally, advice on lifestyle management.

For organisations without the facilities of an occupational health department, there are external agencies who can provide a range of health promotion programmes. Evidence from established health promotion programmes in the USA have produced some impressive results (Karasek and Theorell, 1990). For example, the New York Telephone Company's Wellness Programme designed to improve cardio-vascular fitness saved the organisation $2.7 million in absence and treatment costs in one year alone. Stress management/lifestyle programmes can be particularly useful in helping individuals to cope with environmental stressors which may have been identified by the organisation, but which cannot be changed, e.g. job insecurity.

Tertiary prevention

An important part of health promotion in the workplace is the detection of mental health problems as soon as they arise and the prompt referral of these problems for specialist treatment. The vast majority of those who develop mental illness will make a complete recovery and will be able to return to work. It is usually far more costly to retire a person early on medical grounds and recruit and train a successor than it is to spend time easing a person back to work.

Counselling

Organisations can provide access to confidential professional counsel-ling services for employees who are experiencing problems in the workplace or personal setting (Berridge, Cooper and Highley, 1991). Such services can either be provided by in-house counsellors or outside agencies in the form of an Employee Assistance Programme (EAP). EAPs provide counselling, information and/or referral to appropriate counselling treatment and support services. Such services are confidential and usually provide a 24-hour contact line. Charges are normally made on a *per capita* basis calculated on the total number of employees and the number of counselling hours provided by the programme.

Counselling is a highly skilled business and requires extensive training. It is important to ensure that counsellors have received recognised counselling skills training and have access to a suitable environment which allows them to conduct this activity in an ethical and confidential manner.

Conclusion

As Alistair Mant suggested in *The Rise and Fall of the British Manager* (London, Pan, 1977) "a great deal of what wants doing in this naughty world seems to be reasonably obvious to men and women of goodwill and common sense everywhere. But we have not, it seems mastered the trick of creating the intervening institutions that help us to get things done. We rush headlong from analysis to action, without stopping *en route* to build sound constitutional structures to support our endeavours". We must view employees as individuals who have needs, personalities and commitments outside organisational life and begin to realise (and put into practice) our intuitive feeling that the performance, efficiency, and satisfaction of an employee is linked to total life experience. As John Ruskin said in 1871 "in order that people may be happy in their work these things are needed. They must be fit for it, they must not do too much of it, and they must have sense of success for it".

3. HUMAN RESOURCE PERSPECTIVE ON MANAGING STRESS

3. HUMAN RESOURCE PERSPECTIVE ON MANAGING STRESS

Jose Pottinger

Introduction

Take writing this chapter for example. How to factor the work into an already hectic schedule and avoid adding stress? The answer was to take a week's holiday, I thought, somewhere in the sun with a relaxing and therapeutic environment. So I am sitting here now with the waves gently lapping the shore and the sun caressing the terrace where I'm working. It sounds idyllic, doesn't it? That is not the whole picture however!

The final day before this week's "working therapy", which I had planned to be a "put desk in order day", turned out to be a nightmare, with non-stop telephone calls, no lunch and a multitude of "must dos". Furthermore my hand luggage probably weighed more than my suitcase due to the excessive paperwork, and I shall no doubt feel the need to telephone the office at least once just to make sure all is well. There is no pressure on me to do so. I am not indispensable, and my colleagues will manage supremely well in my absence, though they will have to work harder. I know I will return after this week to a foot of paperwork and post, and several screens of e-mail. It will probably take me several days to catch up but as least this chapter has been written!

I am sure this scenario of manic activity before a holiday followed by an accumulated workload on return has a familiar ring to it. Stress has become very much part of the modern day idiom. Unfortunately the word itself tends to be used solely in the negative sense, yet there is a level of stress in every company. Indeed a reasonable level of stress or pressure helps performance. Take the example of the athlete—the stress before a race causes adrenaline to be released, which turbo-charges the individual to succeed. In the work context the buzz before a particularly important presentation or the excitement of completing a piece of work to a tight deadline, each in its way helps to maintain the momentum within the organisation.

Yet it is when this pressure or stress becomes acute and prolonged that the problems occur and distress follows.

It is a reaction to excessive pressure or responsibility when an individual feels inadequate and unable to cope. The difficulty for companies is that there is no foolproof way of predicting who is likely to be so affected by such pressures. Mental ill-health is indiscriminate and we should therefore not make the assumption that it is only the chief executives who suffer from this condition called stress.

There is quantum evidence now available that demonstrates that the problem exists throughout our organisations at every level to a greater or lesser degree. The physical symptoms of stress are well documented elsewhere in this book. Each individual has a different tolerance curve which determines when stress becomes distress and this curve may vary in different situations and different stages of the life curve.

The cost

Notwithstanding the cost to the individual and their family there is the overall macro cost which impacts on companies and the overall economy. In an age where there is such a keen focus on cost control and profitability the following data should capture our attention.

- The Department of Health in its "Health of the Nation" booklet identifies that three out of ten employees will have a mental health problem each year.

- The Health and Safety Executive estimate that 80 million days are lost each year through mental illness at a cost of £3.7 billion per annum.

- It is also estimated that upwards of 40 million days are lost each year through stress-related disorders at a cost of £1.2 billion per annum.

- In 1991 the European Commission conducted a survey of £13,000 European workers. 56 per cent of the respondents considered that stress at work affected their health.

For some personnel practitioners there may be barriers to tackling the problems of stress. The macho environment or even one of denial may prevail and, by raising the issue of stress, personnel may be perceived in the context as woolly liberal thinkers. Armed with the above data and combined with appropriate internal statistical analysis a cogent business case can be put forward providing the imperative to address the problem.

The bottom line impact cannot be ignored and the benefits of an open and structured approach to dealing with stress can have a significant effect on overall morale within an organisation with consequent impact on effectiveness and performance.

The effect of working and social environmental changes

So what has been happening in the working and social environment to produce such statistics?

During the 1980s and 1990s we have witnessed an accelerating rate of change. In fact change is now a continuum and no longer are we able to pause and draw breath after each elemental step. The need for such change has been prompted by a fiercely competitive environment within the market place transcending to a global stage, with the emerging markets in Asia and the Pacific Rim presenting a real challenge.

The ability to compete in the latter part of this century depends on an organisation's ability to respond to increasing customer demands and requirements. The high performing organisations will not sequentially manage cost, quality and delivery but will simultaneously manage these elements.

The need for cost control, cost reduction and improved profitability have been catch words of the 1990s.

As part of this thrust organisations have flattened structures resulting in fewer levels of management in order to promote environments which create more challenging work assignments, with a higher degree of involvement, thus maximising the utilisation of the skills and talents of their employees. The fact that delegation of decision-making is being passed to the most appropriate level within the organisation, that is to say closest to where the work is being carried out, produces a new set of dynamics and fundamentally changes the previous psychological contract.

To effect these changes without providing the appropriate level of support and development to those affected can produce situations where individuals feel unable to cope. Additionally the flatter organisations significantly alter the concept of the career ladder. Individuals see no opportunities for consistent advancement at least as measured on the previously understood scale. The "delayering" of organisations, as it has come to be expressed, has for many come to be perceived as fewer people doing more work, whereas the intent surely has been to drive improvements in effectiveness, that is to say working smarter not harder.

In the industrial context we have seen the emergence of the knowledge worker, no longer the manual worker. To be fully effective companies must harness the talents of all employees.

The consequential impact on jobs, be it in the context of less jobs or restructuring, as a result of this change process has created uncertainty and insecurity, two factors which can produce a stressful environment.

Notwithstanding this turbulence there has also been a dramatic shift in the technological environment. The type of equipment that is deployed has become far more sophisticated. Computer integrated manufacturing systems, networked word processing facilities, electronic mail, the Internet, have significantly changed the way work is carried out. To comment on it is not to belie the benefits but more to highlight the changes employees have been required to cope with. It has necessitated learning new skills and techniques which for some can be a daunting, even threatening, prospect.

Computer literacy is now by and large a mandatory skill. The emergence of the information age is both exciting and stimulating, but at the same time the ease of passing information and the indiscriminate distribution lists can often result in information overload. One of the key complaints to be heard from managers is the amount of reading they have to get through.

The ability in this environment of change, with all the consequential pressures, to balance home and work life becomes increasingly challenging. The emergence of dual earning homes, single-parent families, and the dilemmas when children are ill can produce acute pressures. Are our personnel policies sufficiently well developed to match this sophisticated environment of change which leads to so much stress? What action can be taken?

Action which can be taken by management

Organisational diagnosis—the symptoms

In order to prepare the business case, it is necessary to gather data internally within the organisation to identify whether a stress problem exists.

There are now tools widely available, notably the Occupational Stress Indicator, which can be administered by an occupational health department or personnel department in consultation with a psychologist. This tool provides a useful profile and highlights particular areas where stress may be occurring; it can be obtained from NFER Nelson. Additionally, stress audits can be administered. One such audit tool can be obtained from the Health Education Authority, and can help to identify not only sources of stress at work and the vulnerable employee but also may provide relevant data covering employee job satisfaction. However, before deploying such mechanisms it is worth referring to some of the more rudimentary data that is generated within organisations which may provide insights as to what is happening and where potential problem areas may exist. Data which may be symptomatic and therefore aid diagnosis are:

- increased absenteeism—at a macro level if attributable to a specific area this may highlight a pressure point for the organisation;

- increased accident rate;

- deterioration in quality performance;

- reduced job performance;

- increased people turnover—the converse of this in times of unemployment is equally a problem since individuals become trapped in an organisation;

- increases in employee relations problems;

- work addiction—people working excessively long hours or even just being present at work to comply with group mores.

All of the above are indicative of problems, be it low morale, poor organisation of work, overload, or poor working relationships, etc., within the organisation; but may also be symptomatic of stress. Care must be taken not to jump to conclusions, but to use the data wisely to prompt further investigation to identify the root causes. It is worthwhile to keep in mind that it is the root cause or causes that require to be treated, not the symptoms. It should also be borne in mind that having obtained the relevant data, it is necessary to establish an appropriate strategy and corrective action plan. Failure to take action on problems identified following the conduct of a stress audit could leave the company exposed should legal claims be brought.

Discovering the possible root causes

There are many possible factors which can create a stressful environment, and generally it is a question of degree. The factors can be divided into two groups, such as:

Physical factors—examples of these are:

- extremes of noise;
- extremes of temperature and humidity;
- poor ergonomics i.e. poor organisation of the relationship between individuals and their machines or working environment;
- hazards perceived or real;
- proximity to toxic or dangerous materials.

Most of these are relatively easy to identify.

Psychosocial factors—this second group of factors, commonly referred to as psychosocial, are more complex. Brief descriptions of some of them are given below.

Organisational culture
It may be that the culture of the organisation is not conducive to effective performance. This may occur through inconsistency between what the leadership says and what actually happens in practice. It may be a culture that works purely on the "Theory X" approach to people management and as such fails to provide the opportunity for people

involvement. The "Theory X" approach was developed by the late Douglas McGregor, and embodies the notion that the average human being has an inherent dislike of work, avoids responsibility and, as such, must be coerced and directed. This type of culture was found in many organisations following the scientific management movement in the 1960s. We would probably label this a "command and control" type of environment which allows little opportunity for participation in the decision-making process, and restricts the ability of the individual to have any influence or control over their sphere of operation.

The organisational culture may be one which embraces erroneous value systems such as the admiration of overwork. Whilst there is a need to create an environment and culture that sponsors employee commitment and contribution, this must encompass a balanced approach. In Japan they have a term to describe the syndrome of obsessive overwork; it is called "*Karoshi*" or death by overwork. *Karoshi* is a documented ailment in which people develop illnesses and die from high stress and the pressures of long working hours. The Japanese officially recognised *Karoshi* as a fatal illness in 1989.

Lack of appropriate leadership
Our expectations of any leadership group are that they will establish strategy and provide a clear sense of direction as to the goals that need to be achieved. Failure to do this leaves employees operating in a vacuum, unsure of how to focus their own performance.

Job/task design and role
The significance of role or task design is a key element. Building too little into the work such that it lacks variety or challenge can be as detrimental as a role or task which is unrealistic in its span of control or content. Both scenarios can produce pressures.

Similarly, role ambiguity and the lack of clarity as to what is required of any individual results in uncertainty. Individuals can feel confused by conflicting demands which leads to role conflict. This, as we have described earlier, can contribute to stress.

Individuals who consistently work within roles dealing with illness, human suffering, violence, danger or even death will be subject to a high degree of emotional demand. This in itself places particular pressures on people, as we have seen with social services and the National Health Service.

Excessive workload and pace
It is quite reasonable to set goals and targets for individuals which provide stretch, but these should be realistic and achievable.

Difficult interpersonal relationships at work
Bullying by peers or supervisors, personality conflicts, inconsistent management styles and perceived unfair treatment of subordinates can all contribute to the creation of pressure.

Work/home interface
The inability to manage effectively the balance between work and home, for example, the difficulties of an inflexible work schedule when a family member is ill and requires attention, will naturally produce tension and pressure.

Job insecurity and lack of career development
Job insecurity and the lack of career development have become key sources of stress during the 1980s and 1990s as the impact of headcount reduction programmes and major restructuring has taken its toll.

The above factors represent the key potential sources of stress within any organisation. It is the degree to which they exist and their impact on any individual which should concern us. Clearly companies can not directly influence the stress caused by domestic circumstances, nor would it seem that restructuring or redundancy will disappear from the agenda of organisational life, but in all the scenarios portrayed above there are very positive and constructive responses that can be made.

While the question of the employer's responsibilities is dealt with in detail elsewhere in this book, it may be useful to include a reminder in this chapter of basic duties.

Employer's responsibilities—basic duties

An organisation which fails to protect an employee from exposure to stress at work may find itself facing a claim for compensation.

Whilst stress is not specifically referred to, employers have a duty under the Health and Safety at Work Act 1974 to ensure so far as is reasonably practicable, that their workplace is safe and healthy.

Under the Management of Health and Safety at Work Regulations 1992 (SI 1992 No 2051) employers are obliged to assess the nature and scale of risks to health in their workplace and base their control measures on this assessment.

It is urged that stress should be viewed in the same context as any other health hazard and although it may be considered to be more complex, a process should be developed which facilitates the identification of risks so that appropriate and effective control strategies can be deployed.

The responses—prevention is better than cure

The Institute of Personnel and Development (IPD) in its guide on occupational health and organisational effectiveness comments that "Properly managing occupational stress will be one of the major functions of organisations in the next decade". The IPD believes that:

- people work more effectively if they are managed in a participative way;
- people will be better motivated if the work experience satisfies not only their economic needs but their social and psychological needs;
- attention to the design of jobs and work organisation improves individual motivation and so leads to greater efficiency.

Let us now turn to specific actions which can be taken. Although there is no one magic panacea, the emphasis should be on the prevention of stress by eliminating the potential root causes. Actions to be taken once damage has occurred fall very much into the remedial and rehabilitation category. In respect of responses to aid prevention, to coin a phrase, it is very much back to basics. Good management practice can create a healthy organisational climate which improves morale, aids performance and can significantly reduce or eliminate potential causes of stress.

Suggested responses are detailed below.

Organisational culture and leadership

- Make use of employee attitude surveys to identify improvement areas. Such surveys may be constructed to focus on key dimensions such as:
  - leadership capability
  - safety
  - environment
  - provision of training and development.

- Put into effect a system of upward appraisal to ensure that appropriate feedback to the manager/supervisor is available which may provide data to assist in the improvement of leadership style.

- Ensure that there are effective and robust communication systems that communicate information and data affecting employees in their work environment. These should embrace the communication of good as well as bad news. A lack of information, particularly when it is self evident that there are problems in an organisation, generates uncertainty and potentially stress.

- Encourage appropriate leadership styles which in turn encourage employee involvement; and the delegation of decision-making to the most appropriate level in the organisation. Good leadership marshals a cohesion in the workforce by establishing common goals and actions that reflect the words.

- Ensure there is effective and frequent communication of the organisation's vision and values.

- Take action to provide a consistently open climate where stress can be talked about in a positive and supportive manner and not carry a taboo. Such a climate should embrace the notion that stress is an organisational issue not only a personal problem.

- Provide training to managers and employees to equip them with the skills to develop an awareness of stress and thus aid early detection. The creation of an organisational climate which provides a social support framework to those who may be affected by stress is invaluable because it leads to a swift and efficient response which can minimize problems.

The type of support framework envisaged is one where the manager or supervisor takes an interest in their employees as individuals and, as such, is able to detect any changes in behaviour which may be indicative of an underlying problem. Such an environment would also consist of an individual or individuals e.g. someone in the personnel department or the occupational health nurse who has the respect, integrity, approachability and necessary skills to offer counselling to individuals. Training to recognise the symptoms that may be indicators of stress are appropriate for such individuals, and will assist in early detection and the necessary actions to prevent exacerbation of the problem to the detriment of the individual and the organisation.

Job/task design and role
Management should:

- Design jobs and tasks which are realistic and provide employees with a measure of control over their destiny e.g. mutually agree workplans and provide training in problem solving tools. Whilst the organisation will determine what needs to be achieved, the individual should have some latitude over the mechanisms of achievement.

- Encourage utilisation of people's talents, use minds as well as physical capacities. Design work to be interesting and challenging. Where technology has simplified the process build knowledge elements into the role to engage peoples' minds, and try to build in variations where repetitive work is involved, e.g. through periodic switching of tasks, involvement in continuous improvement, or problem solving teams. It may also be that in a team-based work system environment which deploys the star concept, individuals may take a leadership role for one of the points on the star e.g. health and safety, training, quality, materials, or such other lead as is appropriate for the organisation.

- Be clear and ensure the employee is clear about the expectation of any job or role. In an age where the key drive is for flexibility, it is not necessary to develop hugely detailed job descriptions which often constrain individuals in the deployment of their skills. An overall statement of responsibilities should suffice. Documentation of the work process will provide the framework needed for quality performance—this can be a simple set of instructions developed by the job holder, or in complex manufacturing plants, process instructions developed by industrial engineers.

- Provide individuals with the necessary training and development to ensure they have the capability to meet the requirements of the job/role. This should apply across the board throughout the organisation.

- Introduce a performance management system to ensure that performance expectations are clear and objectives jointly agreed. Such a system should provide the ongoing opportunity for quality time to discuss and review performance matters, which should be aimed at building confidence, developing strengths and identifying difficulties early in order to enable corrective action to be taken.

This would also assist in minimizing any possible stressful elements.

- Deploy thorough recruitment and selection processes to ensure an appropriate fit between the job/role and the individual who is to carry it out.

Excessive workload/pace

To avoid excessive workload or pace, management should:

- Establish appropriate review systems to ensure that continuing expectations are realistic.

- Introduce continuous improvement programmes which equip employees with the problem solving skills to analyse their work and eliminate those tasks which do not add value. "*Kaizen*" meaning "for the good" or "gradual unending improvement" is a useful technique in this context.

- Encourage a healthy exercise regime. Regular exercise causes the body to release endorphins which reduce stress and anxiety and improve concentration. Some companies have their own fitness facilities, whilst others seek to negotiate group rates at a local gym. Where organisations have sports and social clubs it is often possible to run regular exercise or aerobics classes and sporting activities which not only alleviate stress but also help to build good personal relationships between staff.

Interpersonal relationships at work

It is vital for the efficiency of the whole enterprise to ensure good interpersonal relationships at work. This can be greatly assisted by:

- Provision of qualified counselling support either internally or through an employee assistance programme (EAP) which provides external confidential counselling support. Advice on how to provide this can be obtained from the Employee Assistance Professional Association (EAPA).

- The establishment and communication throughout the enterprise of a treatment policy which sets clear standards and expectations in terms of how employees should behave and relate to one another. Such a policy would deal with the question of harassment in whatever form, bullying, etc. It should also provide a clear procedure for individuals who wish to make a complaint, ensuring the necessary sensitivity, confidentiality and supportive framework in such situations, and avoiding the need to go through an immediate superior, where this person could be the cause of the problem encountered.

- Providing skills training for individuals or team members to help them deal with potential or actual conflicts.

- Similarly, assertiveness training may sometimes be appropriate, as it can provide much needed assistance to individuals who may otherwise by virtue of their disposition, find it difficult to stand their ground and present their case. Advice as to where this type of training may be available can be obtained from the Industrial Society. We may not always like the people we work with, but it is possible to find ways of working together more effectively with the appropriate tools and techniques.

- Establishing grievance procedures for individuals who feel they have been unfairly dealt with.

Work/home interface
Difficulties at home can affect employees in their work environment, so managers should consider the following in particular:

- The creation of a climate whereby individuals feel able to discuss particular difficulties with their manager and be assured of a fair and supportive response.

- Where appropriate the introduction of flexible working policies. In this modern age of technology, telecommuting or allowing individuals to work from home connected by a computer network generates a whole new series of possibilities for the future, though clearly this will not be an option in many environments which rely on synchronous processes. One should not lose sight of the fact that this type of working in itself may also produce its own pressures due to lack of immediate social interaction e.g. it can increase "home" pressures, lead to loneliness and a lack of the immediate support of other employees in terms of advice or encouragement. Indeed the IPD recently commented that whilst telecommuting can be a family friendly form of working, it is not suitable for everyone. Isolation is probably the major disadvantage from the employee's point of view and managers also need to develop new approaches to supplement the lack of face-to-face interaction that is simply not possible in such a regime.

- Leave of absence policies which are known to all employees, and which may usefully support individuals at times of personal crisis such as bereavement.

- Provision of crèche facilities or summer programmes to assist employees with children during school holiday periods.

Occupational health programmes
This is an area which tends to be forgotten by managers—but which I suggest is most important, and should be actively considered. I would like, therefore, to address the very positive and all embracing contribution that can be secured through the provision of an occupational health programme.

The World Health Organisation definition states that "the Occupational Health Service is to promote and maintain the physical, mental and social well being of all staff".

Given the definition above, occupational health programmes are about positive and constructive interventions which may range from the promotion of healthy lifestyle issues in the workplace, and appropriate dietary advice, to provision of healthy menus in the canteen. Basic level health monitoring can also form part of the service with an opportunity for employees to have regular health checks covering weight, blood pressure, urine checks, etc. Such a service has a key role to play in the area of stress when there is the facility to receive qualified counselling support, and timely referral for specialist treatment as necessary.

Such a service can be an internal service for the larger organisation, or in the case of smaller companies, there is now the opportunity to negotiate arrangements with local trust hospitals, or even to develop a shared arrangement with other small companies in the area.

The nature of an occupational health programme provides a positive and powerful message to employees. There is no one overall blueprint, as it will vary according to the needs of each organisation. However, because of the focus on promoting and maintaining the physical, mental, and social well-being of all staff, it can make a very significant contribution to the overall effectiveness of the organisation. It is not simply nice to do, it offers a way of reducing costs associated with ill-health and injuries and in so doing provides the opportunity for improving employee performance.

An example of an Occupational Health Policy can be found in Appendix 1.

Under the umbrella of an occupational health policy, appropriate stress management programmes can be provided. I would caution against a "knee jerk" reaction that suggests the deployment of such programmes is the first and only response in the event of stress being identified within an organisation. It is important to understand the issues and root causes of identified stress and then develop an appropriate strategic response, an element of which may be a stress management programme.

Stress management programmes would embrace training for employees who wish to take action which can help or alleviate stress. An understanding of potential causes and ways in which their effect can be reduced can form part of the training. Additionally, such programmes may provide training in relaxation techniques and the effective use of massage or musical therapy.

In respect of massage some organisations are now using freelance individuals who are members of the on-site Massage Association. Based on a 1,500-year-old form of Japanese acupressure, the massage focuses on the stress release points of the body, neck, shoulders and arms. It is received fully clothed and seated in a specially designed chair. Since the massage takes approximately 20 minutes such sessions can be conducted during lunch or break times thus reducing interruption to the normal work day.

There are many forms of alternative therapies such as aromatherapy, reflexology etc. Whilst to some organisations these may seem faddish, access to these therapies can help provide a comprehensive infrastructure for employees.

In all cases appropriate and preferential rates may be negotiated on behalf of the employees.

The actions listed above are by no means exhaustive, but highlight some of the basic practices that are frequently neglected, and which when deployed appropriately can significantly assist in reducing or eliminating potential sources of stress.

The deployment of the responses listed above are by no means prescriptive, and each action needs to be considered in the context of the particular organisational needs of the enterprise concerned.

Dealing with individuals suffering from stress—how an employer can assist

For those employees who are absent from work as a result of stress it is important that there is an appropriate support framework in place in the organisation for which they work. The individual will no doubt find the experience difficult, and it may therefore be appropriate to maintain a level of personal contact with the individual perhaps through the provision of home visits by the occupational health nurse, if the enterprise has one, or a personnel representative in order to reinforce the support from the organisation.

Such visits require careful consideration and sensitive handling, since it is necessary to avoid exacerbating the problem where it is work-related.

Once an individual reaches the stage where return to work is being contemplated, it is appropriate to arrange a return to work interview to establish whether the individual is ready to return to their job. Advice should then be sought from the organisation's occupational health physician or company doctor. It may also be appropriate to consider a phased return, allowing the employee the opportunity to work part-time until the necessary adjustment has been made.

Continued liaison and regular follow up interviews with the employee, the company doctor and the line manager are essential.

Critical in the whole process is an audit and evaluation of the environment in which the individual had been working, in order to identify and correct the root causes of the problem. The case of John Walker (see Chapter 2 above) is a clear reminder of this necessity. This has generated a great deal of media speculation and fears that employers will be increasingly vulnerable to claims from employees who are suffering stress. The facts in the case (set out here again for ease of reference) are that Mr Walker worked in the social services department in an area with a high and increasing workload in relation to child sex abuse. The combination of nature and volume caused distress. Due to budget restraints no additional resource was available to help. Mr Walker complained, but to no effect and he eventually suffered a nervous breakdown as a result. He later returned to work, where no change had been made to the mode of operation, and he then suffered a second nervous break-down which left him permanently unable to carry out his duties. It was found that whilst the organisation could not reasonably have foreseen the first breakdown, they were liable after the second breakdown since by this time the employer could not argue that the risk of injury was unforeseeable as it had happened before, and nothing had been done to change the conditions which caused the problem.

Final thought

The approaches outlined in this chapter are intended to provide a practical overview of the issues and responses that should be considered when seeking to develop an appropriate strategy to deal with stress in an organisation whether before or after it occurs.

The cost benefits of such a strategy are clear and do not rest on the notion of damage limitation, but focus firmly on the improvements to overall organisational performance and effectiveness by the deployment of good management practice.

One final thought from a personal perspective is the importance of humour in the workplace.

In researching this chapter I found a very interesting article in *Training and Development* (April 1994) entitled "Overcoming the Overdoing" by Lisa Reinhart and Elizabeth Danziger. In this article ways to overcome overwork were listed. The final suggestion was to "lighten up" with a comment about the need to find absurdity in difficult situations. The suggestion was made that we should look for ways to help people take themselves less seriously. It is certainly true that one needs to know one's own culture and tolerance levels. The importance of humour should not be forgotten and the person who can present a serious subject and lighten it with humour is invaluable.

In this age of change and uncertainty, where a considerable proportion of our life is spent at work constantly seeking to make improvements and responding to the next challenge, there is a danger that the intensity and seriousness will become too ferocious, and we must never lose the capacity for humour, which has a unique way of breaking the tension and correcting the sense of balance. When we have lost the capacity for humour, our ability to maintain a balanced outlook will be diminished.

Finally, and most significantly, it is important to treat employees with dignity and respect and to recognise that each employee is an individual not simply a resource. To adhere to this value will greatly enhance the effectiveness of an organisation.

As the great philosopher Plato espoused "only by exercising balance and temperance will I achieve a happy and harmonious life".

4. AN OCCUPATIONAL PHYSICIAN'S EXPERIENCE OF WORKPLACE STRESS

4. AN OCCUPATIONAL PHYSICIAN'S EXPERIENCE OF WORKPLACE STRESS

David Moore

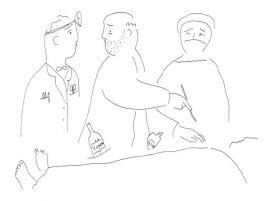

"Don't worry I'm really cutting down now"

Introduction

"See, said they, what you brought yourself to by work, work, work! You persisted in working, you overdid it, Pressure came on, and you were done for! This consideration was very potent in many quarters, but nowhere more so than among the young clerks and partners who had never been in the slightest danger of overdoing it."

These words were written by Charles Dickens in 1857 (*Little Dorrit*). Despite Dickens' probably not being very clear as to the distinction between high blood pressure and "pressure/stress" it would not be unreasonable for the modern reader to conclude that the quotation illustrates two truths about stress at work: it is not new and those who make most noise about it are rarely suffering it. These facts are worth remembering when trying to cope with the problem in a doom-laden atmosphere of disaster, threatened lawsuit and self-serving media hyperbole.

Stress at work

What do we mean when we use the phrase "Stress at Work"? First, what do we mean by "stress"? There is a multitude of definitions and much confusion with "pressure". Indeed some use the two terms synonymously. As far as this chapter is concerned, stress is defined *as existing wherever levels of pressure are inappropriate for optimum work performance and health, and where "pressure" represents the nature and extent of the psychological impact of work, relationships, health and events on the individual.* This is a practical and empirical definition that is unlikely to impress a psychologist but does have the virtue of relating pressure directly to work performance and of making it clear that too little pressure is as likely to damage performance as is too much.

Stress at work: using the definition above, stress can arise from work itself or from factors outside work. Does the difference matter? Perhaps not in a therapeutic sense. But in stress prevention and especially in legal liability, the distinction is important and is sometimes overlooked. An employer, as part of his general duty of care to his employees, must try to prevent stress arising from work. He has every humanitarian, economic and operational, but not legal, reason to do his best to cope where that stress, although manifested at work, is the result of outside factors. Of course, in practice, these two sources of stress hardly ever occur singly and there is always, sooner or later, a dynamic relationship between them. From a company perspective, therefore, it is self evident that measures to be taken fall into two interdependent categories: those directed at work-generated stress and those directed at the amelioration of the effects of stressors external to the company. This, in a sense, is a vertical integration. A horizontal element is represented by the difference between measures directed at the group and those directed at the individual. Recognition that this matrix exists is essential to the understanding of the problem and its solution. The occupational physician in his involvement with the affected individual must operate within it. He must also have sufficient detachment and vision to be able to stand dispassionately outside the whole when making objective recommendations to company management on those policies and procedures that will govern the group.

The stressed workforce—recognition and "diagnosis"

How can a stressed workforce be recognised? First, recognition should not be confused with diagnosis. The patient goes to the doctor because he knows he is ill. He has already recognised illness. The doctor's job is to determine the nature of his disease—diagnosis—and to advise him how it may be cured. The first problem with stress is that individuals and organisations often do not know they are sick. So how are they to find out? In short, someone must look.

Most of the group or institutional signs of high stress levels in a working population are well known: rising sickness absence, employee relations difficulties, product quality problems, anecdotal evidence of individual cases and so on. These are useful in that they show the possible presence of a stress problem in the group, that is, they provide recognition, and if that problem's existence is established may be used as an empirical indicator of its progress (but see below). Unfortunately, useful as these indicators are as warning signs, they are of little use in determining the dynamics of causation—or "diagnosis". To begin with, as phenomena their causation is always multifactorial. It is not even safe to assume that stress is involved at all. Even where stress is a factor it may pale into insignificance compared with, for example, major dissatisfaction with pay. Of course, one can say that pay dissatisfaction causes stress hence the observed effect, but this is rather an unhelpful conclusion, tantamount to saying that all life events cause stress. In other words the major weakness of the indices is that they are a manifestation of association rather than causation. This may seem an unnecessarily pedantic distinction, but without knowledge of *causation* remedial measures cannot be designed and implemented. In fact, the indices give little qualitative information unless they are observed over a period of time. But with time everything changes and is the observed change in the index in question quite what we believe it to be? Some organisations merely treat this difficulty as a "black box": it exists; never mind that of which it consists. Once this conclusion has been reached the options are to do nothing or to treat the symptoms. The former is unacceptable for the legal and other reasons already given. The latter is the "Band Aid" approach— and the "Band Aid" is usually an employee assistance programme (EAP)—of which more will be said later. Rational *preventative* action is not possible. The "black box" may have several levers and buttons in view—but no-one knows which one to pull or press, nor what effect such action may have.

Not only is this approach unfocused and therefore wasteful and uncertain in its effect but, like doing nothing, it will not fulfil the employer's duty under law referred to above. Treatment of the effects of stress is not enough. There must be an effort made to identify its causes and eliminate or ameliorate them as far as is reasonably possible. In this respect stress is no different from any other workplace hazard.

"Diagnosis" in practice—a stress audit

These causes are discoverable by means of a special study or "stress audit". This study should pose the questions: who, whom? (with apologies to Lenin), where, how much, what, and why? To use health and safety legislative terminology the audit is, in effect, an assessment of hazard and, to a degree, a definition of risk. The target population is easy to define: the whole workforce of the company or, in a large organisation or group, a stratified random sample of employees of the major operating companies. All grades of employee must be included (the myth that stress is confined to high flyers and Type A managers is dying but not yet dead). The instrument of the study is usually that time-honoured tool: the questionnaire. This must be chosen carefully for suitability for the workforce in question and of course must be validated and completed or administered in such a way so as not to invalidate it (for example, by ensuring that the instructions for completion of the questionnaire are standard and observed in all cases). A good example of such a questionnaire that the author used with success is the Occupational Stress Indicator, devised by Professor Cary Cooper and his colleagues (Cooper, Sloan and Williams, 1988). Use of this questionnaire in an organisation will answer the questions posed above. It will establish an overall measure of stress that can be compared with data from other companies and thus provide a peer comparison. It will highlight varying stress levels within the company between divisions or departments. It will identify the employee groups at most risk. Most importantly for prevention: it identifies the factors causing stress.

It does have limitations. The first is inherent in all questionnaires. It illustrates the situation only at the time of administration, that is, in epidemiological terms it measures point prevalence—both of cause and effect—and time alters both. The second is confidentiality. A questionnaire distributed by an employer to employees containing many personal questions and giving the opportunity to criticise company culture, management, systems and operations is inevitably an object of suspicion. Respondents are uneasy too at the thought that their superiors may in some way become party to their private feelings. The opportunity that the questionnaire affords to give a gloves-off opinion of one's employer at that employer's own instigation is such an unusual and unlikely experience that those advocating it may be seen as *agents provocateurs*. Finally, the questionnaire itself is formidably long and, for some, difficult to understand.

Initial questionnaire

But it does work. In the author's case most problems were avoided by leaving the sample identification, questionnaire administration and analysis to an academic partner, in this case the School of Management Studies at the University of Manchester Institute of Science and Technology (UMIST). The Company had and sought no access to completed questionnaires nor did it know who had completed questionnaires and who had not. To be able to give assurances to employees that this was indeed the case was vital to the success of the study.

Briefing employees on the purpose and nature of the study proved difficult. The difficulty was partly practical, in getting access to large numbers of people in diverse locations, partly because of residual worries about confidentiality and partly because of employee cynicism concerning the reason for the study. Did the Company really care? Was it just covering its own back? Was the questionnaire merely a device to get rid of people—to weed out the disaffected? Against this background of distrust and to secure employees' acquiescence and an acceptable response rate it was important that the briefing carried conviction as to its purpose and that those giving it had credibility with their audiences. In the first instance and solely for reasons of accessibility, personnel managers were used. With the benefit of hindsight this was an error. Personnel managers' usual briefing tasks are more often concerned with unwelcome news on restructuring and job losses. In short, they were seen, however unfairly, to be part of the problem, not of its solution. The response rate was poor. A second briefing was done using Company Occupational Health Advisers (OHAs) together with personal involvement of the researcher from UMIST. This briefing emphasized a promise to provide personal feedback to those who wanted it. Despite some further vicissitudes it was much more successful and a statistically satisfactory response was achieved.

Analysis of results

The results of the study were quite simple:

- The Company had rather higher levels of stress than the mean of a group of companies previously studied.

- Stress levels were virtually uniform at all grades of employee.

- Stress levels were similar in all areas studied.

- External "locus of control" (i.e., lack of opportunity to use personal initiative) was an important stressor.

- Feeling undervalued and a perceived lack of opportunity for personal development were reported as stressful.

- Perceived shortcomings in communication were reported as stressful.

Action

Action was, in theory at least, as simple as the results. A steering group of four people (a senior line manager, a senior personnel manager, a researcher and the author) was set up to consider the results and make recommendations to the Board. The recommendations included:

- acknowledgement that a problem existed and that remedial action was needed;

- formulation of a policy on stress;

- management training in the manifestations and management of stress in the people for whom they were responsible;

- the provision of stress education or "awareness" for employees;

- continuing stress monitoring.

The Board agreed the recommendations and the Occupational Health and Safety Services (OHSS) department of the Company was given the job of implementing them.

The Policy

The process of implementation started, logically enough, with policy formulation. A policy on stress was drafted and discussed with senior line and personnel managers. The Policy first defined stress for policy purposes. It then identified the principles that were to be adopted in dealing with the stressors that the audit had highlighted and in making clear the action needed to minimize or contain them. Prominent was the requirement to adjust workloads where they were inappropriate and where it was possible, and where "adjust" could mean increase as well as decrease. Managers were urged to invest individuals with value by giving them as much control over their work and circumstances as was possible—and consonant with their abilities. Opportunities for personal development and achievement were to be maximized and attention was to be paid to effective communication.

There were specific innovations:

- stress levels were to be monitored from time to time;
- information on stress, its causes, remedies and pertinent Company procedures was to be given;
- stress awareness seminars were to be made available to all employees, and managers were to be trained in recognition and handling of the stressed employee;
- specialist referral arrangements were made available for affected employees.

These were formidable requirements that in their discharge demanded much planning and administration and consumption of considerable resources of management time and money.

Stress awareness seminars

By far the biggest undertaking was the provision of stress awareness seminars for employees of all grades. These seminars were one hour sessions delivered by the Company Occupational Health Advisers to groups not exceeding eight in number, and were wholly non-didactic in nature. The OHAs, who had been especially trained for the task, acted as facilitators of a group discussion. The discussion had the objective of increasing understanding of stress, its effects and symptoms, learning simple stress relief strategies, including how and where to seek help if affected, all set against the background of the Company Policy. In addition, the seminars were designed to allow the expression of thoughts and feelings and, to some degree, to give the opportunity to let off steam with impunity. They therefore partook something of the nature of group therapy although there was no explicit therapeutic intent. The principal points brought out in the seminar were contained in a booklet, a copy of which was given to each person attending.

Although not all the workforce could be reached, well over 2,000 employees took part. Every seminar was evaluated on the spot and the progamme achieved an 80 per cent approval rating from employees.

It was very hard work. A pattern soon emerged. The seminar would start with most people saying little and one or two more outspoken and invariably critical persons holding the floor. This phase of overt cynicism was then usually tempered by the interjection of some facts about stress and pressure or about work or the Company from the OHA. A phase of discussion of the assertions and facts then followed with more people taking part. Typically, this discussion was illustrated by the speakers with their personal experience or feelings. These were often expressed vividly and with some bitterness, but any tendency for one individual to overstate his case provoked opposition from one of the others and a reasoned consensus was often reached. Although participants were usually not conscious of the fact, the whole process was cathartic and generally ended with people feeling not only better informed, but better.

Management stress training

Concurrently with the stress awareness seminars, stress training for managers was carried out. The objective of this course was not to tell managers about their own stress but to sensitize them to and inform them of the pressure on their subordinates, how to recognise the point at which pressure becomes stress, how to manage the affected employee and how to get skilled help. The training was carried out to a programme agreed with the Company by a firm of consultant psychologists under contract. Together with the formal training, managers were given a small reference manual and access to a "help-line" facility. Again, the training was evaluated and achieved very high ratings.

Referral arrangements

Clearly while these efforts were being made to contain and reduce stress, employees already affected could not be neglected. A referral system was arranged where the employee could seek help (or be referred by his manager). In the first instance recourse was to the OHA. The OHA's task was to determine those employees who could be helped by simple counselling, which she would then supply, and to refer those with more serious or complicated problems to the

Company Medical Adviser. The Company Medical Adviser had then to assess the employee's condition and make a decision as to whether further help was needed and from which source. Depending upon the doctor's opinion, the employee's condition and, most importantly, the employee's wishes, referral was made to skilled help through the employee's general practitioner or to one of a number of clinical psychologists contracted to the Company.

Initial results

The working population involved in the programme, irrespective of grade, was—and is—predominantly male, middle-aged and long-serving. It was perhaps to be expected that the response would be a conservative one with overtones of suspicion and cynicism—they "had seen it all before". Of course they had not seen it before and this "knee jerk" pessimism was a symptom of the problem the seminars were designed to counter. At anecdotal and individual levels therefore it was gratifying to see much, if not exactly positive at least grudging, acceptance that stress was a problem for some—for there was considerable denial from the tougher element—and that what they had all experienced in the seminar had given them better understanding and had left them better fitted to cope. For others however there is little doubt that seminar discussion of the possibility of improvement in "locus of control", of being more agent than client, was threatening. To these people all was someone else's responsibility. They reserved the right to complain if change did not suit them but were unwilling to take an active part.

Many managers in their "management session" (most had of course attended the seminars as well) seemed to have some difficulty with objectivity. They tended to relate what they heard on management of the stressed subordinate to their own feelings of pressure in relation to *their* superiors, or inverted the cause for concern from that of management of the stressed subordinate to the diffculties and pressure the stressed subordinate laid on them, the managers. The most commonly expressed sentiment was that they felt exposed and needed more support. It was hard to avoid the conclusion that in some respects, and paradoxically, the training, while it might in-directly have helped the manager's subordinates, actually increased the pressure on the managers by making them more fully aware of their responsibilities, both ethical and legal.

Anecdotally therefore, there was evidence of improvement but this improvement was neither universal nor unalloyed with less desirable results. A better and more objective measure was needed not only to attempt to substantiate subjective observation but to discharge the undertaking laid down in policy to continue to monitor stress levels.

Repeat stress audit

About two years after the first stress audit and following the completion of the seminar programme and the management training a second stress audit was done. A different and rather shorter questionnaire was used. Like the first it was fully validated (that is, it had been subjected to a testing process by its originators to ensure it did indeed describe and measure that for which it was designed). It was despatched to the total workforce of the companies involved and this time a statistically satisfactory response was achieved in the first instance. The results were encouraging. Stress levels were generally lower and in some important areas this difference achieved statistical significance. A source of particular satisfaction was that those who had attended stress seminars reported statistically significantly lower stress levels than those who had not.

Employee assistance programmes

Having for the time being got as far as we could with strictly preventative measures it was now time to look at an employee assistance programme (EAP). The employee assistance programme has already been mentioned as a "Band-Aid" solution to stress. This reference was not intended to be derogatory. Employee assistance programmes delivered by reputable service providers are valuable and probably achieve positive cost benefit. But they are essentially therapeutic rather than preventative and for the reasons already given should not be the first nor the sole action in a company. Indeed it seems likely that, under health and safety legislation, a company would not be deemed to have discharged its responsibility to its stressed employees merely by the institution of an EAP. Employee assistance programmes are also quite expensive and may present operating difficulties because of incompatibilities with a company's personnel policies. The latter problem is usually capable of resolution—provided it is recognised before you get to the tribunal! Because of such considerations and particularly because installation of an EAP is likely to be an irrevocable step, no decision has yet been made but the proposal remains under active consideration.

Difficulties in workplace stress management—an overview

In dealing with the problem of stress in industry, experience shows that the financial and operational difficulties are negligible by comparison with the people problems. Both managers and workers have their own characteristic vices that are often a severe hindrance to a stress control programme and, perhaps more importantly, will tend to discredit it unless the programme manager is alive to the possibilty. These vices are summarized (and only slightly tongue-in-cheek) in the paragraphs which follow.

Management: some managers rather resemble zoo-keepers. That is, while they are reasonably kind to their animals (subordinates) and see they are fed and watered, they do not in their heart of hearts believe that they are of the same species as themselves. This lack of empathy often makes this sort of manager a stressor in his own right, almost independent of circumstance. He will never realise that others may feel just as he does but differences of intelligence, personality, education and culture may make their expressed response to stress unlike his. With other managers empathy may be felt but suppressed, particularly by those who regard stress as a "rite of passage"; classically from one grade of management to another ("we've all been through it"). Some confuse empathy with sympathy and deny the existence of the condition because they do not wish to appear weak, sympathy being interpreted as weakness—although it is rather hard to understand why this should be so. Paradoxically, this phenomenon is often observed in stressed managers. (The man, who with quivering lip tells you *he* is not stressed and despite a string of casualties does not believe in the existence of the condition, therefore how could there be a problem in his area of responsibility? "But of course, there's been a lot of work recently—and that strike in the machine shop. . ."). Many managers believe that stress is not a blue-collar problem but is a condition confined to high-flyers like themselves. This is a specific and common version of the zoo-keeper syndrome already mentioned.

Some appear personally immune to pressure and utterly incapable of realising that others do not share their good fortune. Some simply do not care: the psychopathic may be met with in all walks of life. Worst of all are the ostentatious, the heart-on-sleeve "carers" who believe that the route to advancement is through what you say rather than what you do; whose insincerity is blindingly obvious to their subordinates and who are stressors *par excellence*.

Employees: the principal employee vice is to blame all performance failures or disciplinary infractions on stress. Too often in cases where the idle, careless or incompetent are under threat of discipline for poor performance, the employee goes sick and the manager receives a "Med 3" from the employee's GP annotated "stress" or "depression". The manager (not being a member of the groups mentioned above) reproaches himself for insensitivity. This mood often does not last but despite the manager's efforts there typically ensues a lengthy period of sickness absence which in the worst cases is characterised by an uncritical and partisan advocacy of the employee's case by the family doctor or psychiatrist. In some organisations this culminates in a wholly unjustified retirement "with honour" on health grounds. In organisations with more management skill and backbone there is either a return to work and efficiency or discipline takes its course.

There is a considerable overlap with alcohol problems. How often are employees seen with performance or disciplinary problems due to drink whose response is that they only drink because they are stressed by their circumstances? Stress is the culprit—and it is always someone else's fault. When the circumstances are investigated one may find typically that the employee is in debt, he was lost his driving licence and his wife has left him and is suing for maintenance. It is stressful certainly but the drink problem is the cause rather than the result of the mess.

This brief overview of employee vices, like that of the management vices, has been simplified to make the point. In real life they are rarely quite as clear cut and there is more than a little "chicken and egg" about them. Managers seeking the answer to the classic question, "which came first?" should seek the advice of the occupational physician. They will find that early discussion of their problem children may well help them to avoid injustice, being taken advantage of, unnecessary disciplinary hearings and lost cases at Industrial Tribunals.

Conclusion

Stress in industry is a substantial and growing menace. It threatens the individual with loss of mental health, welfare and, too often, livelihood. It threatens companies with reduced efficiency, loss of valuable people, lawsuits and possible criminal prosecution. It is, no doubt, a fashionable complaint and provides a useful stick with which to beat companies, authority in general or any body or persons of which or of whom the *cognoscenti* disapprove. Some people deny its existence on these grounds alone, forgetting that there never being wolves at the sheep when the boy cried "Wolf!" is no proof of the non-existence of wolves. The author has seen far too many painful and all-too-concrete examples of stress casualty to be a non-believer.

This chapter describes a systematic attempt to define, prevent and control stress levels in a large group of people at work together with the provision of help to those already affected. Time, the thief, and his helpmate Change have already neutralised much of our good work and we will soon have to repeat in different guise some of our more successful initiatives. But this is an occupational physician's experience.

5. THE LEGAL IMPLICATIONS FOR EMPLOYERS AND EMPLOYEES OF WORKPLACE STRESS

5. THE LEGAL IMPLICATIONS FOR EMPLOYERS AND EMPLOYEES OF WORKPLACE STRESS

Elaine Aarons

"You can't possibly be ill I've got to go to work."

Introduction

This chapter examines stress at work in its legal context. Due to increasing media coverage of this subject, employees have quickly become alert to the potential for them in claiming work-related stress. They are raising stress as an issue with increasing frequency despite the effect this may have on future employment prospects; one would have thought that highlighting a vulnerability to stress would deter employees from raising the issue but in countless cases this does not appear to be the case. Employers are therefore rightly concerned that stress will be raised increasingly often and that they are vulnerable to claims as a result.

Against this background, we examine the common law, statutory and contractual obligations of employers towards employees in respect of stress-related physical and psychiatric illness and follow this by suggestions for minimizing such liability. We shall then consider stress as an element of discrimination claims, and, finally, fair and unfair dismissals.

Employer's duties

Common law duty of care

An employer is under a general duty to take reasonable care to ensure the health and safety of its employees whilst they are at work.

The employer should:

- provide a safe place of work;

- provide safe equipment;

- provide safe and competent fellow employees;

- provide a safe system of work.

The employer owes a duty of care to ensure the above is maintained and may be liable in the tort of negligence if it breaches that duty of care and the employee suffers as a result.

The employer is liable for reasonably foreseeable risks to its employees which means that the employer will be liable if it does not take reasonable steps to eliminate risks that it:

- knew about; or

- ought of have known about.

This common law duty of care covers the physical *and mental* health of employees. The House of Lords held in *Page* v *Smith* [1995] 2 All ER 736 that there is no general justification for regarding physical and psychiatric injury as different types of injury.

This means that an employer may be equally liable for an employee who suffers a mental breakdown as a result of overwork/stress as it would for an employee who suffers physical injury as a result of defective machinery. Stress/overwork should therefore be treated in the same way as any other health hazard.

The care that the employer must take to avoid liability for mental injury through stress/overwork will vary according to the circumstances of the case in question. Consequently, the crucial test is whether the employer can reasonably foresee that his or her conduct will expose the employee to the risk of personal injury, whether physical or psychological. The law does not, however, compensate merely for normal human emotions such as distress, sadness, grief or stress responses short of physical or mental illness.

The main obstacle for employees when pursuing claims that the employer breached its duty of care to provide a safe place or system of work is proving that the mental injury concerned was *caused* by the employer's negligence. With individuals experiencing increasingly stressful home lives with rising divorce rates, escalating exposure to the risk of violence and so on, attributing stress-related illnesses solely to workplace stress becomes increasingly difficult.

Application of the law in decided cases

In the case of *Gillespie* v *The Commonwealth of Australia* [1991] 104 ACTR 1 the employee was a diplomat working for the Australian government. He was appointed to the diplomatic mission in Caracas, Venezuela and suffered a nervous breakdown which he alleged resulted from the negligence of his employers in posting him to Venezuela. He alleged that the living conditions in Venezuela were such as to cause him hardship, that his employers should have informed him of these hardships and that they did not take any steps to relieve him of the various stresses to which he was subject.

In this case the court had no difficulty in deciding that a duty of care was owed to the employee and in considering whether or not the employers had discharged their duty to take reasonable care for the employee's safety, what had to be considered was whether it was reasonably foreseeable that the employee was more susceptible to psychological harm than an ordinary member of the diplomatic staff at Caracas.

The court decided that the discharge of the employer's duty to take reasonable care for the safety of its employees required that any officer posted to Caracas be given some preparation beyond that which was appropriate to a less stressful post, but that the employee's particular vulnerability was not foreseeable. The possibility that an officer would suffer such an extreme reaction as this employee in fact did was remote and reasonableness did not require the employer to give more than the most general of warnings and a description of the circumstances of the post. The court found, however, that the employee was an ambitious man and on the evidence any warning or description was not likely to have deterred him from accepting the post and causation was not established.

In *Petch* v *The Commissioners of the Customs and Excise* [1993] ICR789, CA, Mr Petch joined the Civil Service in 1961. He was regarded as a "high-flyer". By 1973 he had received accelerated promotion to the rank of Assistant Secretary and was put in charge of the Management Services Division of the Customs and Excise. In October 1974 he suffered a mental breakdown which took the form of a bout of severe depression. He returned to work in January 1975 but developed hypomania, a state of euphoria or ebullience which is the opposite side of the coin to depression for those suffering from "manic depressive psychosis". He was transferred from Customs and Excise to the Department of Health and Social Security in June 1975. Mr Petch claimed that Customs and Excise had been negligent in the treatment of him both before and after his mental breakdown. The employer conceded that it owed Mr Petch, "a duty to take reasonable care to ensure that the duties allocated to him should not damage his health". They also accepted that this included the employee's mental as well as physical health but this was subject to the qualification that proving that mental injury was foreseeable, or that it was caused by the employer, was likely to be more difficult in these cases. The judge, defining the test to be applied in relation to the first breakdown, said:

"Unless senior management in the Defendant's department were aware or ought to have been aware that he was showing signs of impending breakdown or were aware or ought to have been aware that his workload had carried the risk that he would have a breakdown, then the Defendants were not negligent in failing to avert the breakdown in October 1974."

On the facts it was found that the employee did not exhibit signs of the impending breakdown and that anyway his workload did not carry a real risk that it would cause a breakdown.

As far as the second breakdown was concerned, the duty of care extended to taking reasonable care to ensure that the duties allocated to him did not bring a repetition of his mental breakdown of October 1974.

The Court of Appeal said that what had actually happened to Mr Petch was not a repetition of severe depression but a bout of hypomania which had contributed to Mr Petch becoming a serious disciplinary problem. The Court concluded that the employer had not been negligent in its treatment of Mr Petch during this period as it had done its utmost to persuade him to take sick leave and seek medical help and did as much as it could have reasonably be expected to do so to dissuade him from working. The Court found that the transfer to the DHSS was a sensible solution to an intractable problem. Accordingly, the employee's claim failed.

Much of the recent interest in cases involving stress at work has been generated by *Walker* v *Northumberland CC* [1995] IRLR 35. When first reported it was heralded in the press as a "landmark" decision. In fact, the case was decided on the well established principles of common law explained above. The judge made comments on this matter in the decision by stating:

"There has been little judicial authority on the extent to which an employer owes his employees a duty not to cause them psychiatric damage by the volume or character of the work which the employees are required to perform ... Whereas the law on the extent of the duty has developed almost exclusively in cases involving physical injury to his mental health, there is no logical reason why the risk of psychiatric damage should be excluded from the scope of an employer's duty of care."

Mr Walker sued his former employers for their negligent failure to provide a safe system of work. He worked for the Council as an Area Social Services Officer between 1972 and December 1987. He managed four teams of social services field workers in an urban area producing many childcare problems and investigations of child abuse. During his employment the population of his area rose considerably putting his department under a lot of pressure. He was a dedicated man. Unfortunately in November 1986 he suffered a nervous breakdown and remained off work until March 1987.

By September 1987 Mr Walker went on sick leave following medical advice and subsequently suffered a further mental breakdown which forced retirement. In February 1988 he was dismissed on the grounds of permanent ill-health. He alleged that the psychiatric damage he suffered had made it impossible for him to resume his career of some 20 years and that he was incapable of obtaining any employment which contained a significant amount of responsibility.

In respect of the first mental breakdown, the court found that the failure of the Council to take any reasonable steps to help Mr Walker with his workload was a cause of stress and anxiety and, interestingly, the judge was satisfied that the first breakdown was caused entirely by workplace stress. However, he did not find that the council had breached their duty of care as on the evidence at the relevant time it was not reasonably foreseeable that Mr Walker's workload would give rise to a material risk of mental illness. The judge noted that cases based on psychiatric damage would "often give rise to extremely difficult evidential problems of foreseeability and causation". He went on to say that this would almost certainly be the case in the realm of professional work which of its nature was demanding and stressful.

As far as Mr Walker's return to work was concerned, he made it clear to his employers that he needed help to cope and he suggested a reorganisation of the social services in his area. This suggestion was rejected but he was told he would have the help of another officer who would be seconded to him for as long as necessary. This officer was later withdrawn. It is perhaps not surprising that the judge had no doubt that the employers should have foreseen that Mr Walker would suffer further mental illness if he was again exposed to the same workload. He found that the employers should have appreciated that he was more vulnerable to psychiatric damage as a result of the first breakdown. The judge said that it was "quite likely, if not inevitable" that Mr Walker would suffer a further breakdown.

Consequently, although the court did not accept that Mr Walker's first breakdown was foreseeable to his employers, it found that the second breakdown was foreseeable and that the employers should have taken appropriate steps to support Mr Walker in his work. There was speculation that the damages that would be awarded would be in excess of £200,000 for the employers' liability for the second break-down; it never got as far as an award of damages being made, however, as the employers appealed against the decision that it was liable and before the appeal was heard the case was settled.

Following *Walker*, it appears that such cases can be successful. However, the floodgates have not been opened by the case. The success of claims for mental injury caused by work stress will depend on all the circumstances of the case. Causation and foresee-ability will often be difficult to establish. As mentioned above, an employee will have to show that the injuries relate to stress at work and have not been caused by external factors, for example, a marriage break-up. It may also be difficult to show that the employer was aware or should have been aware that the employee was likely to suffer from any stress-related injury. At what stage should the employer realise that the employee is at breaking-point? As the court noted in *Walker*, this question is particularly difficult to answer in the context of a professional person working under a great deal of pressure.

Equally, however, it would not be safe to assume that the employer need not take steps to support an employee until the employee has had a nervous breakdown or has suffered from some other stress-related condition such as an eating disorder. Whether or not the risk of a stress-related injury occurring is reasonably foreseeable will turn on the facts of each case. It may be apparent from the volume or stressful nature of the work itself. Alternatively, there may be warning signs, for example higher than usual sickness absences. In circumstances where an employee actually informs the employer that he or she is having difficulties coping with an existing workload then the employer should certainly take reasonable steps to support that employee.

The Health and Safety Executive issued guidelines on occupational stress during 1995 and these are discussed later. The guidelines are intended to target all employers and, as a result of such guidelines, it may well be harder in the future for employers to argue that they could not foresee that an employee was exposed to the risk of a stress-related injury.

When discussing an employee's rights in relation to stress one should be clear to which rights one is referring. The *Walker* case was a claim for personal injuries against the employer. That is a claim that an employee would bring in the High Court or County Court. It is to be distinguished from employment claims generally. Employment claims arise as a result of a breach of the contract of employment or, alternatively, under statutory provisions (e.g. the right not to be unfairly dismissed). In most situations one needs to bear in mind the risk of both a personal injuries claim and other employment claims being made. However, the distinction is important as the considerations regarding what an employer should do when faced with an employee suffering from stress may be different depending on the nature of the claim concerned.

Contractual duties

Employers are under express contractual duties arising from the agreed terms in the contract of employment *and* implied duties which exist regardless of the written terms in the contract of employment and are designed to protect the employee's position in the workplace.

Duty not to injure the health and safety of employees
An employer has an implied contractual duty not to injure the health of its employees and this extends to the psychological health of employees. In the case of *Johnstone* v *Bloomsbury Health Authority* [1991] IRLR 118 the Court of Appeal examined the compatibility of (i) an express contractual term allowing the employer to require the employee to work up to 88 hours a week and (ii) the employer's implied duty of care for the health of its workforce. In the contract of employment the employee had to make himself available for up to 48 hours' overtime at the employer's discretion. The employee alleged

that the hours were intolerable leading to sleep deprivation and damage to his mental health. This had given rise to physical damage in the form of stress, depression, sickness and frequently suicidal feelings. He sought a declaration that his employer was in breach of its implied contractual duty of care for his health and safety and damages for the resulting injuries.

The Court of Appeal expressed the view that there had to be some restrictions on the employer's contractual rights. Although the employee was under an absolute obligation to work the contractual overtime if called upon, the employer in calling upon him to do so was exercising a discretion which must be exercised subject to the ordinary duty not to injure unreasonably its employee's health. The employer could not therefore lawfully require an employee to work so much overtime as would result in reasonably foreseeable damage to the employee's health. Applying this principle, the Court of Appeal found that bearing in mind the length of time that the employee was required to work, and the stress the long hours placed him under, his employers should reasonably have foreseen that he would suffer both physically and mentally. The term in the contract was subject to the employer's discretion; and that discretion was fettered by the implied duty relating to an employee's health and safety.

The *Johnstone* case addressed the issue of an employer's duty of care in the context of its discretionary powers under the employment contract. The question which must be raised is whether in the event of an express contractual term stipulating that 88 hours should be worked, the employer's duty of care is waived by an employee agreeing to be bound by those terms? Is an employee who suffers physical or psychological injury as a result of working excessively long contractual hours barred from arguing that the employer was in breach of its duties as it was a risk assumed by the employee?

It has been suggested by commentators that an employer cannot exclude its liability in this way for a number of reasons:

- If an employment contract expressly or impliedly excludes or restricts an employer's liability for the death or personal injury (physical or psychological) of an employee, it may be that such a term is void under the Unfair Contract Terms Act 1977. This legislation prevents a person from excluding or restricting his liability for death or personal injury caused by negligence in most contracts and extends to employment contracts in favour of the employee.

- An employer cannot contractually exclude his obligation to monitor employee health under the Management of Health and Safety At Work Regulations 1992 (SI 1992 No 2051). The obligation involves identifying and implementing measures to prevent risks to employees' health and safety. Thus, an employer who becomes aware that contractual hours are placing an excessive strain on employees should take steps to alleviate the situation.

- In the case of *George* v *Plant Breeding International (Cambridge) Ltd.* COIT 29560/90, the contract of employment provided that the employee would be "required to work extra hours ... at the request of management, when the workload made it necessary". The employee in question was dismissed after he refused to comply with a request to work for 12 hours a day, 7 days a week for 9 weeks. The IT found that in spite of the contractual provisions, such an order was not a reasonable one. There had to be a limit to the number of hours worked. If the workload demands hours beyond a reasonable time-limit, then steps must be taken to organise the work in some other way. Again however, this case concerned an express term under which the employer had a discretion in relation to the contractual hours it would require the employee to work.

Implied duty not to interfere with or frustrate an employee's proper job performance
An employer must provide appropriate support, training and resources in order to meet its implied obligation not to frustrate or prevent the proper performance of an employee's job. Inadequate supervision, poor communication, and a generally non-supportive environment are all likely to give rise to differing levels of stress in employees.

This is illustrated in the case of *Associated Tyre Specialist (Easter) Limited* v *Waterhouse* [1976] IRLR 386. It was held that it is an implied term of fundamental importance in the contracts of supervisory or managerial employees that they should have their employer's support for their actions in their supervisory and managerial roles. Failure to provide the support systems that enable an employee to carry out his or her role is a breach of the employer's duty.

Lack of employer support was a central issue in the case of *Whitbread* v *Gulyes* [1995] IRLR 509. The applicant was promoted to become manager of a large branch of her employer's business. Due to inappropriate staff support she worked a 76-hour week. Because of this excessive workload, she requested a transfer to another branch. When her request was turned down, she resigned. The Employment Appeal Tribunal (EAT) found her employer to be in repudiatory breach of contract. Its failure to provide adequate support and staff resources had prevented the applicant from performing her contractual obligations to any extent. The EAT also concluded that the employer had promoted the applicant to her job knowing that she lacked the experience to perform the job without proper back-up.

Implied duty to maintain trust and confidence
An employer's implied contractual duty to maintain mutual trust and confidence requires the provision of a reasonable support structure to ensure that an employee can carry out his or her job without "harassment", bullying or disruption by fellow workers.

In *Wigan Borough Council* v *Davies* [1979] IRLR 127 an employee, who had refused to support her fellow colleagues in a work-related dispute, was subjected to a total unwillingness by her colleagues to speak to her and a refusal by them to co-operate with her in her work. Eventually, the situation became so intolerable that she resigned. It was held that the employer had fundamentally breached an express and implied duty to render her reasonable support. The onus had been on the employer to identify reasonable steps to defuse the situation and it had failed to do so.

This case should be contrasted with *Hobbs* v *British Railway Boards* [1995] IRLR 554. In this case the applicant resigned whilst suffering from severe stress because a fellow employee had indecently assaulted his step-daughter. The applicant had applied to the employer to have the accused transferred elsewhere. It was held that the employee had not been unfairly constructively dismissed because the employer had postponed consideration of the applicant's request for a transfer and had decided not to suspend the accused before knowing the outcome of the criminal trial. The employer had taken steps to minimize the contact between the two employees and had offered reassurance and support to the applicant. There had been no fundamental breach of the employer's implied obligation to take reasonable steps to support the employee so as to enable him to carry out his duties.

The question to be decided was not what steps the employer should have taken but whether the action it actually took (or did not take) amounted to a fundamental breach of its reasonable duties to support the employee.

Employers must also be aware of the cautionary tale in *Bliss* v *South*

East Thames Regional Health Authority [1985] IRLR 308 where the employer questioned the employee's psychiatric well-being. The Court of Appeal observed: "It would be difficult, in this particular area of employment law, to think of anything more calculated or likely to destroy the relationship of confidence and trust ... than, without reasonable cause, to require a consultant surgeon to undergo a medical, which was correctly understood to mean a psychiatric examination, and suspend him from the hospital on his refusing to do so".

Statutory duties

There are no legislative provisions in the United Kingdom which deal specifically with the issue of stress and the mental and psychological well-being of employees and workers. However, forthcoming legislation on working time, the provision of the Disability Discrimination Act 1995 which came into force on 2 December 1996 and the Health and Safety at Work Act 1974 together with provisions contained in related legislation and regulations apply to both the physical and mental health of employees. The concept of disability discrimination is dealt with more fully under the general heading discrimination below.

Working time

The Working Time Directive 1993/104/EC was passed into law on 23 November 1993. Member States had three years in which to implement it. The United Kingdom's objection to the applicability of the Directive in the United Kingdom failed (*United Kingdom of Great Britain and Northern Ireland* v *Council of the European Union*, ECJ, 12 November 1996). The Government is currently consulting on the drafting of legislation. The main provisions require Member States to take measures to ensure that (subject to particular derogation):

- every worker is entitled to a minimum daily rest period of 11 consecutive hours per 24 hours;

- in each seven-day period, every worker is entitled in addition to an uninterrupted rest period of 24 hours;

- average working time for each seven-day period, including overtime, must not exceed 48 hours;

- every worker is entitled to paid annual leave of at least four weeks.

There are a number of important exclusions. Under Article 1, the Directive does not apply to air, rail, road, sea, inland waterway and lake transport, sea fishing and other work at sea and the activities of doctors in training. Article 17 provides that the Directive would not apply to managing executives, family workers or workers officiating at religious ceremonies. Further derogations are permitted in respect of security and surveillance activities requiring a permanent presence in order to protect property and persons (e.g. security guards and caretakers) and in activities requiring continuity of service or production (e.g. hospitals, postal and telecommunication services, ambulance and fire services and gas, water and electricity production). Article 18 allows Member States to opt out of the implementation of the 48-hour week provision on condition that no individual worker is compelled to do more than a 48-hour week without prior agreement and no worker is subjected to a detriment in the event that he or she is unwilling to agree to a longer working week. Even the right to opt out of the 48-hour working week is subject to review by the European Council of Ministers prior to 2003.

This Directive will clearly have a fundamental impact on working practices in Britain. It is also likely to colour the attitude to work-related stress which may be seen in some cases to be inextricably linked to hours worked.

Health and safety
The extensive body of health and safety legislation coming from the European Community is also relevant in this context, in particular the following regulations:

- Management of Health and Safety at Work Regulations 1992 (SI 1992 No 2051) (known as the Framework Regulations);

- Manual Handling Operations Regulations 1992 (SI 1992 No 2793);

- Health and Safety (Display Screen Equipment) Regulations 1992 (SI 1992 No 2792);

- Personal Protective Equipment at Work Regulations 1992 (SI 1992 No 2966);

- Provision and Use of Work Equipment Regulations 1992 (SI 1992 No 2932);

- Workplace (Health, Safety and Welfare) Regulations 1992 (SI 1992 No 3004).

Taken as a whole, the Framework Regulations and the five "sister" Regulations (as they are referred to) which were brought into effect at the same time imposed significant new obligations on an employer. Accompanying these Regulations is an approved Code of Practice issued by the Health and Safety Commission. Approved Codes of Practice and the Guidance Notes issued by the Health and Safety Commission do not have the status of law. However from a criminal point of view, if a provision of an approved Code of Practice is breached, a breach of the law will be taken to have been proved in any criminal proceedings unless the court is satisfied that legal requirements have been complied with, otherwise than by observance of the Code. There is no right of action in any civil proceedings in respect of failure to comply with the general duties imposed on employers by sections 2–7 of the Health and Safety at Work Act 1974 or indeed the requirements of the Framework Regulations but breaches will be relied on as *prima facie* evidence in the failure to carry out required practice and will generally be pleaded in the general allegations of any negligence claims.

Duties of employers under the Health and Safety at Work Act 1974 (the HSW Act)

- Section 2(1) of the HSW Act requires employers to ensure so far as is reasonably practical the health, safety and welfare at work of their employees.

- Section 2(2) of the HSW Act sets out a number of specific duties including the provision and maintenance of a working environment that is safe, without risk to health, and adequate as regards facilities and an arrangement for employees' welfare at work.

These duties imply that an employer must assess the risk to the physical and mental health of their employees and balance this against the financial and practical measures which might be necessary to avert them.

One should note that the definition of a "personal injury" for the purposes of the HSW Act expressly includes "any disease and any impairment of a person's physical or mental condition" (S. 53). The HSW Act does not of course give rise to a claim under civil law but there is a criminal sanction. For example, last year the Health and Safety Executive brought a criminal prosecution against Firth Furnishings Limited following an accident in which an employee's thumb was crushed in machinery. Another employee subsequently suffered a mental illness after witnessing the accident and continuing to work on the same dangerous machine. The magistrates' court found the company guilty of breaches of the HSW Act in respect of both employees, and imposed fines of £2,500 for each offence. The company was also ordered to pay the employees compensation of £2,000 and £300 respectively.

In magistrates' courts, the maximum fine for most offences is £5,000 but for breach of section 2(1) or section 2(2) (amongst some other offences) the maximum is as high as £20,000. Moreover, a six months' imprisonment sentence may also be imposed, for failing to comply with prior notices.

In Crown Courts an unlimited fine may be imposed and a failure to comply with prior notices could lead to a prison sentence of up to two years.

Despite seemingly heavy penalties, in reality convictions are rare. Statistics issued by the Health and Safety Executive in 1992 show that whilst 572 people were killed at work during the year, there are fewer than 150 prosecutions annually for cases of reckless manslaughter.

Risk assessment

In complying with its duties under the HSW Act the employer needs to carry out a "risk assessment". This is now explicitly set out in the Framework Regulations which require employers to make a "suitable" and "sufficient" assessment of "the risks to the health and safety of their employees to which they are exposed whilst they are at work". Some of the sister Regulations also require the employer to undertake a risk assessment. An example is the risk assessment required under the Manual Handling Operations Regulations 1992. Compliance with any duty in the sister Regulations will normally be sufficient to comply with the corresponding duty under the Framework Regulations.

The whole ethos of modern health and safety law is the prevention of personal injury, whether physical or psychological, by risk assessments whose purpose is to identify the preventative or protective measures which an employer needs to take to comply with his general and specific statutory obligations. Thus an employer should:

- review risk assessments if there is any reason to believe that they are no longer valid or if there has been any significant change in the matters to which they relate;

- record the significant findings of such risk assessments where the employer employs five or more employees;

- comply with obligations on employers relating to pregnant workers so that employers should include in their risk assessment, an appraisal of any risk which might be posed to a new or expectant mother or to her baby from working conditions;

- ensure provision of such health surveillance as is appropriate having regard to the risks identified by any risk assessment. The approved Code of Practice indicates that appropriate health sur- veillance procedures can include medical examination which may involve clinical examination and measurement of physiological or psychological effects by an appropriately qualified practitioner.

Ill-health
Ill-health resulting from stress caused at work should be treated in the same way as ill-health due to physical causes present in the workplace. The employers have a legal duty to take reasonable care to ensure that health is not placed at risk through excessive and sustained levels of stress arising for instance from such things as the way the work is organised and the way people interact with each other at their work. Employers should therefore be bearing stress in mind when assessing possible health hazards in the workplace and keeping an eye out for developing problems. They must also be prepared to act if harm to health seems likely.

Stress-related illnesses or conditions may be connected with certain physical characteristics of the working environment. The Workplace (Health, Safety and Welfare) Regulations 1992 cover a very wide range of matters including:

- effective and suitable provision for ventilation;

- sufficient quantity of fresh or purified air;

- suitable and sufficient lighting;

- sufficient space in work rooms;

- the provision of sanitary conveniences and washing facilities;

- suitable and sufficient rest facilities in readily accessible places.

These Regulations are also supplemented by an approved Code

of Practice and they have applied to new, modified, extended, or converted workplaces (or parts of workplaces) since 1 January 1993.

Ways of minimizing liability for stress

The interview

What is said at interview will set the tone for the future. Will the job that the employee is in fact required to perform match up to that described at interview? The pressure loaded on the employee after commencing employment often bears little relationship to the impression the employee was given of the job before accepting the offer of employment.

The employer should consider at the outset what the job will involve and whether the expectations of what the employee is required to accomplish are realistic. This may be particularly relevant to part-time appointments which are referred to in more detail below.

Legally, there may in fact be more protection to be gained from overstating the job than understating it. If the employee knew at the outset exactly what was involved, then this will be a factor that will be given weight when a court considers a claim where stress is an issue.

Having said this, the real focus for employers at the interview stage will be on how to get the best out of their employees, not on stress. It seems obvious that overloading employees with work is likely to be counter-productive. Moreover, matching employee's skills, experience and temperament to the requirements of the job will be equally important since work-related stress is often caused by the employee's shortcomings in competence or capability.

Job description

The job description will provide written evidence of the expectations of the employer. Some thought should be given in drafting a job description as to whether those expectations are realistic; what is the point of a job description which expects too much?

Job descriptions should not be incorporated into contracts of employment, but should be in a separate document which is expressly stated to be non-contractual and is reviewed regularly, perhaps at appraisal time.

Attempting to take the job description outside the contract is intended to reduce the risk of constructive dismissal claims arising as and when the job description is changed. This also has its attractions in relation to stress since it will provide a greater flexibility for the employer to vary the job description if the employee does suffer from stress-related illness. The employer may want to vary the job description in order to minimize the risk of a personal injuries claim. There may be tasks/responsibilities which the employer may wish to remove because of a concern that as a result of the stress-related illness the employee may not be able to exercise appropriate judgement or, alternatively, a history of poor attendance may mean that certain tasks are undertaken by somebody who the employer can rely on to be at work.

That is not to say that job descriptions that are not incorporated into contracts can be varied in any respect without the risk of comeback. First, there is a complex legal argument that even though the job description is stated to have no contractual effect it in fact does. Secondly, even if that argument fails, there is always the risk of the employee resigning and claiming constructive dismissal when his or her role diminishes to the extent that this could affect status, remuneration, or opportunities for career development or if there are issues that go to the root of the relationship of mutual trust and confidence between employer and employee. Such constructive dismissal claims are not easy from the employee's point of view (not least because to claim constructive dismissal the employee has to resign and therefore lose his/her job with all the uncertainties that brings regarding how long he/she will be unemployed) but equally there are many cases where such claims have succeeded. If the job description is expressed to be non-contractual, however, whilst the employer is not guaranteed that it will have an absolute defence to a constructive dismissal claim, depending on the facts it may strengthen the employer's case.

During employment

If an employee is being overworked, badly managed or under-supported, this should be seen by the employer in the same way as if he or she was operating a defective machine or working with dangerous materials without proper safety equipment.

The Health and Safety Executive has published a guide for employers on combating stress in the workplace. If employers follow these guidelines, stress at work will be "nipped in the bud" and, therefore, grounds for stress claims will disappear. The following suggestions are a summary of the guidelines.

- Employers need to establish procedures to ensure that the problem of stress at work is understood and taken seriously. Excessive stress should not be seen as a personal problem but an issue which managers, staff and the organisation as a whole are committed to addressing. It is important to ensure that the individuals are not made to feel guilty about their stress problems and are encouraged to seek the relief and support they may desperately need.

- Employers should adopt an effective complaints procedure (similar to that adopted in sexual harassment cases) for employees. There is an implied term in every contract of employment that the employer will provide a proper method of dealing with work-related grievances (*WAR Goold (Peamak) Ltd* v *McConvell* and another [1995] IRLR 516).

- Employers need to adopt effective work management practices to ensure that employees are not given too much work or work beyond their capabilities and capacity. Employees need to feel confident about their work and be given credit for it.

- It is best, so far as is possible, to match the job with the abilities and motivations of the person in it. This might mean giving the person scope to make changes and involving them in any changes the employer might make. It might also mean carefully identifying the requirements of the job and the experience of the person recruited, and offering early training and instruction not just in dealing with the new job but in the working environment and the particular pressures to be found.

- Management style should avoid inconsistency, indifference or bullying.

- Employers should recognise that people cannot cope easily with prolonged periods of uncertainty.

- The things that can help remove unnecessary stress are confidence and competence, consistency of treatment, and good two-way communication. These should be combined with some flexibility; scope for varying working conditions; an open attitude by managers to what people say to them about their jobs or the stresses of work; ensuring that people are treated fairly and that bullying and harassment of those who seem not to "fit in" is prohibited; and ensuring that all staff have the skills and resources needed to do their jobs properly.

- Employers should be prepared to offer support to staff who are, or are likely to be, affected by stress and the pressures of work. Such support could include:
  - encouraging staff to attend stress awareness or stress management courses;
  - where problems have developed, ensuring that line managers provide support and, where necessary, refer the person for further help;
  - in larger companies, providing confidential help-lines and counselling in-house; and
  - in smaller companies or where problems are severe, encouraging employees to seek medical help.

- Problems relating to stress in the workplace should be monitored, possibly through periodic anonymous staff surveys. Also employers should include stress/overwork in any risk assessment exercise undertaken.

- Employers should incorporate discretionary clauses in employment contracts for employees to work extra hours which are reasonable.

Incentives

Incentive packages in themselves increasingly put pressure on employees. Team-related targets have their positive and negative sides; they may reduce absenteeism and in many cases improve team-building. However for some it will create an additional pressure; not only is the employee responsible for himself/herself and for his/her family, but also he/she is responsible to "the team".

Discretionary bonuses, particularly those that are intended to form a significant part of the employment package, will also be a potential source of stress by virtue of their inherently uncertain nature.

Productivity bonuses and commission only contracts will, again, in their own way, increase the stress on employees—indeed this could potentially be very damaging if the stress evidences itself in pressure selling to the public. This can damage a company's image and its sales to the public who may be put off if the employee exerts too much pressure.

Again, it is a question of balance. Stress is just one issue of many in deciding how to incentivise a workforce. However, it is perhaps one that should be borne in mind.

Senior executives

Particular issues arise with executives who are entitled to longer than minimum notice periods. If they suffer from stress-related illness such that they become unable to perform their duties, what must an employer do? Service agreements may enable the employer to terminate without notice if the executive is absent by reason of ill-health for a prolonged period or for significant intermittent absences. This, often, does not give the employer that much scope. For example, the right to dismiss after absences totalling 26 weeks in an 18-month period would not be unusual. For a Managing Director or Finance Director suffering from stress this is an exceptionally long period for employers to have to wait.

We have not reached the stage where including specific provisions for termination as a result of stress would be acceptable to executives negotiating new service agreements. However, senior executives often have the right to long notice periods and if an executive suffers from a stress-related illness, the only way of dismissing him/her will often be to make a severance payment for the balance of the contract, which, in many cases, can be a significant cost. For moral reasons, an employer may feel that an employee who is stressed should receive payment for the balance of his/her contract, but it will depend upon the culture and philosophy of the employer concerned as to whether or not this is an approach they are prepared to adopt for an employee who is, effectively, failing to perform.

The summary termination provisions in service agreements will often provide for an employer to dismiss without notice if the executive is negligent in the performance of his/her duties or if he/she brings the company or himself/herself into disrepute. These may catch some executives under stress who are not capable of exercising judgement.

In many ways, the executive who is stressed and who battles on at work or who has regular intermittent absences is more difficult to deal with than the individual who is absent long term by reason of stress-related illness. A provision in the contract of employment entitling the employer to require the executive to undergo a medical examination, whether or not the employee is absent from work, is very useful in these situations. Indeed, a caring employer seeing signs of stress may see it as being in the best interests of the employee to refer him/her for medical advice. Better to cure and restore an employee to maximum effectiveness than simply to give up and dismiss. Some care should be taken however in requiring a medical examination; there has been case law which has held that requiring an employee to undergo a psychiatric examination amounts to a breakdown in trust and confidence between employer and employee entitling the employee to claim constructive dismissal.

A particular feature, however, with senior executives is that an employer's threshold for continuing the employment of an individual known to suffer from stress is often significantly lower than with more junior staff and this is because of the greater responsibility that the executive is required to carry. Once an executive is identified as suffering from stress, the employer's perception of that individual may be tainted thereafter. The question of whether or not it is reasonable for the employer to take this stance (i.e. whether the executive has a claim for unfair dismissal) may be of minor importance given the damage the employer perceives that the executive may do to the business due to lack of judgement etc.

As far as terminating the service agreement/contract of employment of a senior executive is concerned, in many cases the employer will not have to prove that the decision to dismiss was reasonable. The sensible employer who decides termination is the only answer will offer a severance package to terminate the employment which will be generous enough to ensure that it is paid in full satisfaction of all claims the employee may bring, including claims for breach of contract and unfair dismissal (to waive unfair dismissal claims there would either have to be a "compromise" agreement signed pursuant to Section 203 of the Employment Rights Act 1996 or staged payments with the final instalment of the termination payment being paid after the time for bringing an unfair dismissal claim has expired and only if a claim has not been made).

Many employers express concern as to whether dismissal increases their exposure if a claim for personal injuries is brought as a result of work-related stress. This question is valid for all employees, not just senior executives. However, it may be more difficult for senior executives to mitigate their loss by finding alternative employment and therefore, if their personal injuries claim is valid, they are more likely to have a higher claim against the employer than might be the case for a less senior employee. Having said this, the executive would have to prove that the stress was work-related in order to be able to claim damages. Provided the employer can show a satisfactory business reason for needing to terminate the individual's employment (e.g. they were ceasing to be effective in the job they were employed to undertake) then the fact that the employer has dismissed the employee is unlikely to provide evidence which will be detrimental to the employer in any subsequent personal injuries claim that is brought. (The risk of a claim for unfair dismissal may be increased if the employee asserts that he/she is suffering from stress because of work conditions; see "Automatically unfair dismissals" below.)

Discrimination and stress

Disability

The employment provisions of the Disability Discrimination Act 1995 came into effect on 2 December 1996 and may well be relevant in this area. It will apply to discrimination on the grounds of both physical and mental impairment which has a substantial and long term adverse effect on an individual's ability to carry out normal day-to-day activities. "Mental impairment" will include a mental illness "only if it is a clinically well-recognised illness". For example, clinical depression arising from stress could fall within the definition. However, the illness must have a long term effect which means that it has lasted for at least 12 months or is likely to last for at least 12 months or, more seriously, for the rest of the life of the person affected. The legislation makes it illegal for employers of 20 people or more to discriminate against an employee on the grounds of his or her disability in relation to the terms of employment, recruitment process, termination of employment, by deliberately preventing him or her access to benefits or by subjecting him or her to any other detrimental treatment. There is also an obligation to make reasonable adjustments to the working environment including the building, equipment and hours of work in order to cater for a disabled person's needs. Failure to do this can result in a claim.

To put this in the context of an employee suffering from clinical depression, it may be discriminatory to refuse him or her work for this reason, or during employment to prevent the employee having time off to attend doctor's appointments or counselling sessions. Employers will need to consider the implications of the duties which the Disability Discrimination Act 1995 imposes when deciding how it should treat employees (or prospective employees) with stress-related medical conditions covered by the legislation.

Sex and race discrimination

Claims by employees for discrimination are very likely to be accompanied by claims for stress. In *Duffy* v *Eastern Health & Social Services Board* [1992] IRLR 251 (a case from Northern Ireland where there is religious and political discrimination which does not apply in the rest of the United Kingdom) a Roman Catholic woman whose employer failed to appoint her to a position to which it appointed at least one Protestant who was less well qualified and experienced than her, was awarded £15,000 for injury to feelings. The Industrial Tribunal found that over a considerable period of time the complainant had suffered "fear, humiliation, frustration, insult, stress and deep hurt arising out of a blatant act of unlawful discrimination".

In sex and race discrimination cases, claims for injury to feelings arise. Provided the employer proves there has been discrimination, the Industrial Tribunal will always consider whether there should be an award for injury to feelings when determining the amount of compensation payable.

As there is now no limit on the amount of compensation that may be awarded, we have been seeing awards creep upwards. Compensation for injury to feelings has increased from the recommended maximum of £100 in 1981 to a number of recent awards in the region of £5,000 to £10,000 and rising. Stress as a reason for increasing compensation for injury to feeling is something that is very likely to become commonplace particularly if backed up by medical evidence. The highest award yet made for injury to feelings is over £28,000. This was awarded in July 1995 to an auxiliary prison officer who suffered racial discrimination and victimisation by the Prison Service (*Armitage, Marsden and HM Prison Service* v *Johnson* [1997] IRLR 162). The Tribunal said they were impressed with Mr Johnson's "forbearance" as he had "been subjected to sustained hostility" for more than three years and "his complaints were ignored or inadequately dealt with".

A recent change of approach by the Employment Appeal Tribunal may curb sums awarded in the future. In *Orlando* v *Didcott Power Station Sports and Social Club* [1996] IRLR 262 an employee was awarded £750 compensation for injury to feelings for sex discrimination. In reaching this figure the Tribunal had regard to a case decided before the compensation limit was lifted. On appeal the employee argued that the case was irrelevant because it was decided before the cap was lifted and that £750 for injury to feelings was a perverse finding because the amount was too low. The Employment Appeal Tribunal found that cases decided before the upper limit was lifted could be used as a comparator if, as in this case, the reference was made to show that an award for injury to feelings was to be made in accordance with the same rules as apply to awards for damages for personal injuries. More interestingly, the Appeal Tribunal held that a figure which was somewhat lower than the minimum amount usually awarded in the particular circumstances cannot ever be said to be perverse.

Sexual harassment

Stress may well be raised by employees who are claiming sexual harassment. If they have drawn the harassment to the attention of the employer and the employer has not responded adequately in the way in which it has dealt with the issue, this may give the employee the opportunity to claim damages against the employer for the stress arising out of the harassment.

The protection that the law provides to an employee who has suffered from harassment is that he/she can make a claim under the Sex Discrimination Act 1975. The employer will be vicariously liable for the harassment carried out by any of its employees in the course of their employment. Moreover, if the employer is made aware of the fact that an employee is being sexually harassed and does not respond, the employer may well also be liable for a personal injuries claim. This will of course depend on the facts of the case and the extent to which the employer could reasonably have expected that stress-related illness could result from the harassment that occurred. However, in more severe cases it is likely that employers would be expected to anticipate some stress-related illness where harassment occurs even if there was no prior history of stress of which they were aware in relation to that particular employee.

All this points to the need for employers to have adequate equal opportunities policies including policies on how to deal with complaints of harassment. Each personnel department should preferably have a member who has been specifically trained in counselling techniques and who specifically deals with harassment complaints.

Part-timers

It has now become accepted that legally part-timers should be treated on an equal footing with full-timers. The Employment Protection (Part Time Employees) Regulations 1995 (SI 1995 No 31) have given part-timers the same employment protection rights as full-timers. This arose because it was accepted that there is a predominance in the part-time workforce of women and that treating part-timers less favourably than full-timers is discriminatory (*R* v *Secretary of State for Employment, ex parte Equal Opportunities Commission* [1994] IRLR 176, HL).

Part-timers have always complained that they do more, proportionally, than full-timers. This may become an increasing feature of discrimination claims, if, indeed, part-time employees are having to put in significant amounts of overtime in order to fulfil their job description which the full-timers in the same organisation are not having to do. This, again, may be combined with stress-related complaints, particularly given the setting where women are trying to combine childcare and domestic responsibilities with work.

Interestingly, the recent case of *Helmig* v *Stadt Lengerich* [1995] IRLR 216 made it clear that it was not discriminatory to refuse to pay overtime rates to part-time women when full-timers were paid such rates when they worked overtime. The case is illogical if the function of overtime is to reward employees for giving up their own time. Arguably overtime is more disruptive to a part-time employee than it is to a full-time employee and there can be no objective justification for the part-timer not to be rewarded on at least the same basis as the full-timer for hours worked over and above contractual hours. It is probably only a matter of time before a part-timer brings a claim for discrimination and stress as a result of the unrealistic expectations the job demands when measured against the agreed contractual hours.

The practical consequence of this is, as with all messages above, to be realistic as to what one expects a part-timer to do. The significance is that since there is no compensation limit on sex discrimination claims, and with the risk of a claim also being made for personal injuries as a result of stress-related illness, a cultural change in the attitude to what employers expect from part-timers is urgently required. Progressive organisations will already have set realistic expectations for the work required—it is the smaller, or "bottom line" orientated, organisations that are probably most at risk in this regard.

It should be added that the issue of a discrimination claim arising as a result of demands to work overtime may also be brought by women working full-time. Again, this could be combined with claims for the stress caused due to juggling work and domestic responsibilities.

Dismissal

Employees who are dismissed have two sets of rights:

- contractual rights;
- statutory rights.

Where an employee is dismissed for stress-related reasons, the employee's contractual rights are usually only to receive notice or to be paid in lieu of notice. It is worth noting that employees who are dismissed whilst absent by reason of sickness are entitled to receive salary for the equivalent of their statutory minimum notice period even if they have exhausted their rights under any company sick pay scheme (Employment Rights Act 1996).

A contractual claim could arise for failure to follow the company's disciplinary procedure if the employee's dismissal is for performance rather than ill health reasons. It will be a matter of construction as to whether or not the employee has a contractual right for the disciplinary procedure to be followed.

As far as statutory rights are concerned, employees who have been employed for two years or more have the right not to be unfairly dismissed. An Industrial Tribunal considers the issue of unfair dismissal in two stages:

- was the dismissal for a permitted reason?
- was the employer acting reasonably in treating that as a sufficient reason to dismiss?

The tests that Industrial Tribunals have developed to determine whether the employer acted reasonably in treating that as a sufficient reason to dismiss are set out below.

As to dismissal due to either persistent brief absences, or long term absence, all the facts of the case will be considered by the Industrial Tribunal in deciding whether the dismissal was fair. In *Spencer* v *Paragon Wallpapers Limited* [1976] IRLR 373, Phillips J said "the basic question which has to be determined in every case is whether, in all the circumstances, the employer can be expected to wait any longer and, if so, how much longer?"

In that case the circumstances listed which ought to be considered were:

- the nature of the illness;

- the likely length of the continuing absence;

- the employer's need to have the work done which the employee was engaged to do.

In *Lynock* v *Cereal Packaging Limited* [1988] IRLR 510, Woods J said that the key words were "sympathy, understanding and compassion". Woods J added the following to the above list:

- the likelihood of the illness recurring or some other illness arising;

- the length of various absences and the spaces of good health between them;

- the need of the employer for the work to be done by the particular employee;

- the impact of absences on others who work with the employee (e.g. the call on them to work overtime);

- the extent to which the difficulty of the situation and the position of the employer has been made clear to the employee so that the employee realises that the point of no return, the moment when the decision to dismiss may be taken, is approaching.

Other factors which are relevant in deciding whether a dismissal is fair will be:

- whether the need for an employee with robust health is especially strong;

- whether the size of the business cannot tolerate the absence i.e. the work cannot be readily absorbed by other employees;

- the impact on team-related bonuses.

It has been made clear that these cases are not cases in which warnings are appropriate—the correct approach is one of under-standing.

The Industrial Tribunal will balance the needs of the business and those of the employee. The Tribunal will wish to be satisfied that the employer has tried to resolve the problem in a reasonable manner. It will wish to see that the employer has carried out an investigation so that he is sufficiently informed of the medical position.

The decision in *Martin* v *British Railways Board* (1991) (S) EAT 362/91 illustrates the need in all cases for an employer to carry out an adequate initial investigation into an employee's apparent conduct problems. Mr Martin was dismissed for being drunk at work after his shift manager noticed that he was slurring his words and had glazed eyes. Mr Martin explained during an internal appeal against his dismissal that he was suffering from hypertension, the symptoms of which could be mistaken for drunkenness. The Appeal Tribunal held that the dismissal was unfair because the employer should have carried out further investigation after the internal appeal hearing to discover whether Mr Martin's condition was in fact due to ill health.

The Advisory Conciliation and Arbitration Service (ACAS) advises that even where it is established that an employee is suffering from alcohol or drug abuse, employers should consider whether it is appropriate to treat the problem as medical rather than a disciplinary matter. Furthermore, such "problems" could be merely symptoms of some underlying stress-related condition.

Medical examination

In most cases the employer will need both to consult the employee's doctor and also ask the employee to submit to a medical examination. In order to apply for a medical practitioner's report, the employee's consent will be required in a manner consistent with the provisions to the Access to Medical Reports Act 1988. In brief, the legislation requires:

- an employer not only to notify the employee of the intended application but also to inform the employee of his or her right to withhold consent to making the application;

- if the employee gives consent, he or she is entitled, at the same time, to state that he or she wishes to have access to the report before it is supplied;

- once the employee has had access to the report, it will not be supplied to the employer unless the employee gives consent, *or* 21 days beginning with the date of the making of the application has elapsed without any communication from the employee;

- before giving consent, the employee may request the medical practitioner to amend any part of the report which he or she considers incorrect or misleading;

- if the medical practitioner is not prepared to amend the report but the employee still wants to submit it, the practitioner must attach a written statement giving the employee's views if the employee requests it.

Employers are not expected to set themselves up as medical experts. The decision to dismiss or not to dismiss is not a medical question but a question to be answered in the light of the available medical evidence. Whilst in some cases an Industrial Tribunal may consider consultation with the employee alone adequate, it is best practice to seek medical evidence and not simply to rely on consultation with the individual.

If the employee refuses to be medically examined, the employer will not be able to compel him/her to undertake an examination. For instance, in *Bliss* v *South East Thames Regional Health Authority* [1985] IRLR 308 a consultant surgeon made a successful constructive and unfair dismissal claim against his employer who purported to compel him to take a medical examination in the absence of an express or implied contractual power. The facts were that after a breakdown in relations with another consultant at the same hospital, the plaintiff consultant was evaluated by a three-man committee in accordance with established procedure. The committee found that there was no mental or pathological illness. The Court of Appeal concluded that the employer only had an implied power to demand a medical examination if it had reasonable grounds for believing that the consultant might be suffering from physical *or mental* disability which might cause harm to patients or adversely affect the quality of their treatment and due to the findings of the committee this was clearly not the case.

In instructing a company doctor it is important that the doctor is provided with all the relevant material. In *Ford Motor Co. Limited* v *Nawaz* [1987] IRLR 163, the Employment Appeal Tribunal said that it was not enough for management to act on the opinion of their medical advisers. They would have to go further by carrying out a proper investigation through their medical practitioner in order to satisfy the requirements of a fair dismissal. An employer will have only investigated the matter properly if the medical practitioner has sufficient material before him upon which to advise management.

Where an employer is faced with conflicting medical advice, provided he is acting reasonably, he will not necessarily be acting unfairly if he accepts the report which is less favourable to the employee and this results in the employee's dismissal (*Singh-Deu* v *Chloride Metals Limited* [1976] IRLR 56 and *Jeffries* v *BP Tanker Co. Limited* [1974] IRLR 260). The dismissal was deemed to be fair in *Singh-Deu* even though a specialist had concluded that the employee, who had been suffering from a mental illness, had recovered and was, therefore, fully fit to return to work. The conflicting opinion of the company doctor was preferred by the Tribunal because the specialist could not give an assurance that there would be no recurrence of the illness and it was thought that the company doctor was in a better position to appreciate the nature and importance of the employee's job from the safety aspect.

It will only be in the most exceptional circumstances that a dismissal will be fair despite the fact that there has been no consultation. In *Eclipse Blinds Limited* v *Wright* [1992] IRLR 133, a registered disabled employee with a heart complaint had worked for the employer since 1978 as a receptionist. She was an excellent employee although her health deteriorated over time and sickness absences increased. She eventually became part-time and her attendance showed signs of improvement. However, there was subsequently further deterioration resulting in her giving the company's personnel officer a 13 weeks' sick note. She agreed to the personnel officer contacting her GP to find out her prospects of resuming work after the sick note expired. The GP wrote back to say that there was no possibility of her returning to work in the near future.

Although temporary staff had been employed during the absences, given the GP's comments, the company reluctantly decided to seek a permanent replacement for the employee and to dismiss her. The company knew that it was desirable to consult with her but were concerned that she did not realise the seriousness of her condition and that if they discussed this with her, they might disclose information about her health of which she was unaware. They therefore simply wrote to her explaining that due to ill-health she was being dismissed.

She subsequently brought a claim. The case went as far as the Court

of Session in Scotland. The court accepted that in normal circumstances employers would have been expected to consult with the
employee before dismissing her but that this situation arose through
the employers' genuine concern to avoid giving the employee information about her health of which she was unaware. The Tribunal's
finding that the employers had not acted unreasonably in dismissing
without consultation was upheld.

Fair dismissals

There are situations where an employer may dismiss an employee
fairly if an employee is suffering from stress-related problems directly
or indirectly caused by an employer's business. This will always be
subject, however, to the dismissal not amounting to discrimination
under the Disability Discrimination Act 1995.

Stress could provide grounds for dismissal in a number of ways:

- it may result in the employee being incapable of doing the job
  because the nature of the job itself brings about the illness—a
  normally robust employee would be able to cope with the stresses of
  the job, but not this employee;

- intermittent absences through illness may result in an unacceptable
  level of attendance leading the employer to the conclusion that
  dismissal is the appropriate course;

- the employee may have an extended absence through ill-health as a
  result of which there comes a point when the employer can fairly
  dismiss;

- stress can cause inadequate standards of performance in which case
  for a fair dismissal it will be necessary to be able to demonstrate
  that the employer took steps to alleviate the stress. There are no
  decided cases on whether it is appropriate to follow a disciplinary
  procedure.

Application of the law in decided cases

The Employment Appeal Tribunal, however, ruled in the case of *G. W.
Netcom* v *Whitwell* (1994) (unreported) that it may be fair to dismiss
an employee where continuing to work could give rise to personal
injury to the employee. In this case Miss Whitwell was dismissed after

being absent from work for four months suffering from a disease affecting her hearing and balance. Immediately prior to her dismissal, she said that she had been advised by a hospital doctor that she could return to work if her employer provided her with suitable ear protection. Having consulted the employment Medical Advisory Service, her employers were not convinced that this protection would make any difference and were concerned that if she did return, this might aggravate her condition. The EAT held that in the light of the employer's absence control policy, which only permitted a 16-week period of absence on health grounds, the company had not acted unreasonably in dismissing Miss Whitwell. In the EAT's view, the company was fully justified in deciding not to take the risk of allowing her to return to work to see how she got on, adding that no reasonable employer would take such a risk given the possibility of exposing such an employee to personal injury and therefore exposing itself to potential further litigation.

In contrast, in the case of *Coverfoam (Darwen) Limited* v *Bell* [1981] IRLR 195, a company director who suffered a heart attack was dismissed before he was due to return to work. The employer stated that the dismissal was due to the fact that it feared that the director would sustain a further heart attack following a return to work and that this would constitute a frustration of the contract. The employer's argument was rejected on the grounds that a contract which is still capable of being performed but is subject to an unforeseen risk, which has not manifested itself, is not frustrated. The EAT also went on to say that unless the nature of the employment is such that the risk of illness is of such importance as to make it unsafe for the employee to continue with the job, risk of illness cannot amount to grounds for fairly dismissing an employee.

An employer can take into account the fact that it may be in breach of its contractual common law duty of care in relation to its employee health and safety obligations by allowing an employee back to work when deciding whether to dismiss. This will be particularly relevant where an employer has received medical reports stating that an employee is unsuited for certain types of work and working conditions cannot be altered to accommodate the problem and no suitable alternative employment is available (*Liverpool Area Health Authority Teaching Central and Southern District* v *Edwards* [1977] IRLR 471).

An employee whose psychiatric condition could put fellow workers in danger could be fairly dismissed. If there was medical evidence that the employee lacked judgement as a result of stress and this could harm fellow workers or members of the public this may constitute fair grounds for dismissal (*Harper* v *National Coal Board* [1980] IRLR 260).

The fact that the ill-health has been caused by the conduct of the employer does not necessarily mean that the dismissal of the employee is unfair. In *London Fire and Civil Defence Authority* v *Betty* [1994] IRLR 384 an employee dismissed on grounds of ill-health claimed that he had been unfairly dismissed because of illness that had been caused by his employer's actions. The case concerned a long serving fireman who was accused by his employers of racial harassment and abuse of fellow employees. Following an interview he was told that he would be transferred from his station. Shortly afterwards he suffered a nervous breakdown as a result of the accusations and subsequent events. He never returned to work but was placed on the sick list, and at the end of 1989 he was certified as being permanently unfit for work. In March 1990, following a medical investigation, his employers decided to dismiss him on grounds of ill health. The accusations against him were eventually found to be totally baseless. The employee did not dispute that he was unfit for work or that his employers had adopted a fair procedure in terminating his employment. He did, however claim unfair dismissal on the basis that his illness, and therefore his dismissal, had been caused by the employers' actions.

The Employment Appeal Tribunal stated that in cases involving dismissal for ill-health, the Tribunal's function is to determine the fairness of the dismissal according to the enquiries made and procedures used by the employer, and the employee's medical condition. It is not part of the Tribunal's function to ascertain whether the employee's illness was caused or contributed to by the employer. The employer's duty to act fairly is not affected by considerations as to who was responsible for the illness. A contrary conclusion would require the Tribunal to become involved in an endless dispute over medical matters about which they have no expertise. In many cases it would effectively prohibit an employer who had caused an employee's illness from ever dismissing the employee for ill-health reasons, and it was open to the employee to pursue an action for damages for breach of duty against his employers in the civil courts.

Harvey on Industrial Relations and Employment Law does, however, suggest that where the ill-health was caused by the employer, a Tribunal might expect the employer to demonstrate extra concern before implementing a dismissal (*Parrott* v *Yorkshire Electricity Board* [1972] IRLR 75). The corollary of the principle that an employer can act fairly in dismissing even though his actions caused stress could be used as a basis for dismissing an employee who in the course of a disciplinary procedure goes absent for stress reasons. It will, however, depend on the facts of the case and it will also be necessary to satisfy the Tribunal that no undue pressure was exerted during the disciplinary process that a reasonable employer would conclude could lead to stress.

An employer may find it difficult to claim a dismissal was fair if no steps were taken to try and fit the employee into some other available job. It is not that the employer is required to create a special job for the employee nor find the employee alternative work; but there may be available work which is within the capacity of the employee to do which he or she should be given the chance of doing in the circumstances, even if this involves a reduction in salary and benefits (*Merseyside and North Wales Electricity Board* v *Taylor* [1975] IRLR 60). That is not to say there is a duty to create a job but it is interesting to note that we are not, here, talking about offering "suitable alternative employment". By analogy to the laws on redundancy, the employer may have to consider alternative employment throughout the group of companies of which it is part, although it may be borne in mind that it has been stated that employers are not expected to go to unreasonable lengths in seeking to accommodate someone who is not able to carry out his or her job to the full extent.

However, what is reasonable is a question of fact and degree for the Industrial Tribunal. For example in *Garricks (Caterers) Limited* v *Nolan* [1980] IRLR 259 it was found that the employer acted unreasonably in dismissing an employee when he refused to resume shift work for health reasons without considering in detail whether alternative work could be found. From the evidence, it was clear that there was an alternative job available for the employee and although it involved doing some work which would exacerbate his illness, that work could easily have been done by someone else. Therefore, the company could have easily accommodated the employee.

The case of *McPhee* v *George H. Wright Limited* [1975] IRLR 132 is a good case to illustrate the way in which the matters referred to above should be taken into account. The employee was a warehouseman who had been employed for seven years. He suffered from an anxiety state in August 1974 and was absent from work. After some months the employers said they were compelled to fill his position and wrote to him stating that provided he returned to work by a stated date they would place him in a different department where a vacancy for a warehouseman at the same wage had arisen.

The employee wrote to the employers informing them that he could not return by that date and enclosing a doctor's certificate. The company stated that they were unable to keep the job open and could not guarantee finding a job in another department owing to economic difficulties. The employee was given four weeks' notice of termination of employment. The employee's unfair dismissal claim failed. The Industrial Tribunal stated that where an employee is dismissed because of absence due to ill-health, the firm cannot be expected to wait indefinitely for an employee to return when his work has to be done and there is a need for a replacement. By waiting as long as they did, the firm was considered to have acted as reasonably as could possibly have been expected (they had waited three months). Although this is a 1975 case, the following statement of the Industrial Tribunal is noteworthy: "The more true it is that [the employee's] illness was occasioned by incidents or attitudes at his place of work, the more reasonable it becomes for the company to reach a decision they can no longer employ him".

The Tribunal took into account the length of service but also bore in mind the fact that the work had to be done by somebody, and that at no time was any indication given of a possible return date. They could not keep his original job open but had offered him an alternative. They then had to fill that alternative job because of the employee's continued absence. The dismissal was found to be fair. Again, quoting the Tribunal:

"It has to be borne in mind that [the right to claim unfair dismissal] is designed to provide compensation for certain specific matters, and cannot be used, nor was it intended, to provide an additional source of compensation for any illness, sickness or injury".

It should not be assumed that because an employee's rights under the sick pay scheme have expired that a dismissal will automatically be fair. Equally, it should not be assumed that an employee cannot be fairly dismissed even though he or she still has rights to continued pay under a sick pay scheme. All the factors stated above will be relevant whether or not the sick pay entitlement has expired.

If an employee is unfairly dismissed for ill-health grounds, it will not generally be appropriate for compensation to be reduced on the basis that the employee's incapacity contributed to the dismissal. An employee who persistently refuses to send in medical reports or attend a medical examination may find a reduction is made for his/her contribution to the dismissal. In the case of *Rao* v *Civil Aviation*

Authority [1994] IRLR 240 the employee was dismissed from his job as an air traffic controller. This was found to be an unfair dismissal on procedural grounds, and the case subsequently went to the Court of Appeal on the issue of compensation. The Industrial Tribunal had found that but for the unfair dismissal Mr Rao's employment would have continued for approximately three weeks and there was only a 20 per cent chance that it would have continued after that. There was also found to be contributory blameworthy conduct on his part (involving an application for leave to go to India on a ground that proved to be spurious). The Court of Appeal confirmed that the compensatory award could be reduced to reflect the finding that even if the employers had followed a fair procedure there was an 80 per cent chance the employee would have been dismissed.

Constructive dismissal

Few cases have addressed the question of whether an employer is guilty of unfair constructive dismissal when, as a result of prevailing work conditions, excessive stress has caused an employee to resign.

In a personal injury action a plaintiff employee must establish that his or her employer has been guilty of negligence and is in breach of its duty of care. However, an employee in a constructive dismissal action need not demonstrate that the employer has been negligent; only that the employer is in breach of an express or implied term of the contract. The breach has to be so fundamental, of course, that it goes to the root of the contract of employment or indicates that the employer no longer intends to be bound by the essential terms of the contract. In these circumstances, an employee is entitled to terminate the contract and make a claim. If an employee waits too long before leaving, he may be taken to have allowed the breach of contract by his employer and, consequently, surrendered his right to claim constructive dismissal.

In *Wilton* v *Cornwall and Isles of Scilly Health Authority*, 19 May 1993, CA, an employee who retired from employment following a psychological breakdown caused by the employer's conduct was held not to have been constructively dismissed because she had affirmed the contract by delaying her resignation for almost 18 months. The Court of Appeal accepted the fact that at the time the employee left, the pressure that the employee complained of had subsided and her decision to resign was, therefore, independent of the previous events.

By contrast, a constructive dismissal claim will be valid where an employee has continued to work despite breaches of contract by the employer until the employee "cracks" under a final breach and decides to resign. In *Lewis* v *Motorworld Garages Ltd* [1985] IRLR 465, the employee continued to work after a demotion and change of salary structure, loss of an office to himself, a smaller car and a withholding of a salary increase given to other employees, but finally resigned after a series of criticisms raised by senior management. The Court of Appeal found that, even if an employee had not treated a previous breach of an express contractual term as an indication that the employer no longer wants to be bound by the contract, he is entitled to add such a breach to other actions, which, taken together, may cumulatively amount to a breach of the implied obligation of trust and confidence. This means that conditions giving rise to on-going stress may eventually provide background material for a claim arising out of a final incident. This is known as the "last straw" doctrine.

Although employer's contractual duties have been discussed earlier in this chapter, a few more examples where a breach of express or implied contractual terms can give rise to a claim for constructive dismissal are set out below.

The employers' implied duty of care in relation to health and safety may be breached where an employer fails to provide a grievance procedure. For example, in *British Aircraft Corporation* v *Austin* [1978] IRLR 332, the Employment Appeal Tribunal found that within the health and safety duty, employers "are also under an obligation to act reasonably in dealing with matters of safety, or complaints of lack of safety which are drawn to their attention by their employee". Provided the complaint is "bona fide or is not frivolous" employers should investigate it promptly and sensibly. Similarly, in *WA Goold (Pearmak) Limited* v *McConnell and another* [1995] IRLR 516, an employer's failure to provide and implement a procedure that dealt with two employees' grievances promptly was found to be a fundamental breach of contract entitling the employees to resign and claim constructive dismissal. In the Employment Appeal Tribunal's view, the right to retain redress of a grievance was fundamental for very obvious reasons: the working environment might lead to employees experiencing difficulties due to physical conditions under which they work *or* a breakdown in personal relationships. There might also be difficulties arising out of the way authority and control were exercised, sometimes by people who themselves had insufficient experience and training to exercise such power wisely.

An employer may breach his duty of care for the health and safety of an employee by not only deliberately taking risks but also by failing to prevent risks of which he ought reasonably to be aware. In another "last straw" case, an employee who waited in the cold at the entrance to the factory for 25 minutes resigned making a complaint that during the very cold winter she had to work in "freezing conditions". The Employment Appeal Tribunal rejected the employer's contention that the employee would only have been entitled to resign if she had complained of the cold problem and the employer had done nothing about it, on the reasoning that as the conditions of work were well known to the Managing Director, the complaint was not a pre-requisite to a finding of constructive dismissal (*Graham Oxley Tool Steels Limited* v *Firth* [1980] IRLR 135).

In circumstances where an employee is transferred to work which an employer knows will be detrimental to the particular individual's health, he will be in breach of the implied duty of care. Therefore, if an employer knows or ought reasonably to know that an employee cannot cope with the increase in his or her existing workload, a claim of constructive dismissal will be upheld. Conversely, an employer is not liable for physical or psychological injury resulting from a change of job function which could not reasonably have been foreseen (*Jagdeo* v *Smith Industries Limited* [1982] ICR 47).

Violence at work is another occurrence which can lead to stress-related physical and psychological injury. Under the employers' implied duty of care to health and safety, falls the duty not to expose employees to risk of criminal attacks. For example, in *Evans* v *Sawley Packaging Limited* COIT 2916/15, the employee's claim for constructive dismissal was upheld where an employer failed to take complaints and criminal charges against other employees seriously. Also, in *Keys* v *Shoefayre Limited* [1978] IRLR 476 a shop assistant successfully claimed constructive dismissal following two armed robberies at the shoeshop where she worked. An Industrial Tribunal concluded that any reasonable employer would or should have known that the area was rife with crime, and could easily have discovered this by making reasonable enquiries. To the employer's argument that similar employers in the area also failed to take serious protection against crime, it replied, "we do not think it is fair to say that because of what other people did or did not do in perhaps different circumstances that is proof that the [employers] were excused from taking any steps whatever to secure their staff from the terrifying experiences which the applicant had to go through".

Automatically unfair dismissals

It may be, however, that an employee does not have the opportunity to resign, but is in fact dismissed by an employer for raising a health and safety issue. In such circumstances, a dismissal will constitute an automatically unfair dismissal by virtue of Section 100 of the Employment Rights Act 1996. Section 100 provides that if an employee is dismissed because he or she raises a health and safety grievance with the employer by reasonable means where there is no safety representative or committee, or it was not reasonably practicable to raise matters by those means, such a dismissal will be automatically unfair, regardless of length of service.

It appears to be essential for a Section 100 claim that the employee is dismissed. Resignation will not, it appears, be sufficient for the purposes of section 57A (*Baddeley* v *Mehta* (1995) COIT 46041/94). In the light of *Goold* v *McConnell* (above), however, an employer's failure to address a health and safety grievance may be regarded as a fundamental breach, entitling the employee to claim constructive dismissal under Section 100.

If, by contrast, the employee is punished (other than dismissal) for raising a health and safety grievance, Section 44 of the Employment Rights Act 1996 may be applicable. Section 44 provides that an employee shall not be subjected to any detriment on the grounds that he or she brings to the employer's attention circumstances connected with his or her work which he or she reasonably believes are harmful to health and safety. "Detriment" is defined as any act or deliberate failure to act by the employer.

Conclusion

Despite recent publicity, and the 1990s preoccupation with stress as a workplace issue, the current worry felt by employers that they may face huge compensation claims that are stress-related is quite unfounded. The decision in *Walker*, the case that has sparked off the debate, was not as much a step into uncharted territory as an incremental adjustment to long-established principles of common law. In effect, personal injury claims have merely been extended to include clinical illnesses caused by stress or overwork. As we have seen from the *Walker* case, the issue of foreseeability and causation are high hurdles for the litigant to cross. It will be extremely difficult for an employee to show in most cases that in the particular circumstances his employer reasonably knew he would suffer from stress-related illness or indeed that the stress-induced condition was caused by work rather than extraneous pressures.

This does not mean though that the employers should close their eyes to the issue of stress in the workplace by treating employees like machines with utter disregard for their work capacity or sensibilities. Employers also owe a whole host of contractual and statutory duties to their employees, including those in more senior positions, which are designed to protect health and safety in the workplace. If employers fail to take measures to fulfil these duties they lay themselves open to claims for constructive and unfair dismissal claims and, indeed, under the health and safety legislation even to potential criminal sanctions. Furthermore, with the influence of the European Union, employers are increasingly subject to European employment legislation. It is, therefore, important for employers to take a long term view on stress in the workplace by adopting recruitment and employment policies similar to those suggested by the Health and Safety Executive guidelines to minimize the risk of stress arising in the workplace. Bearing in mind the expense of litigation and that staff turnover and sickness absence related to stress costs employers an estimated £1.3 billion a year in the United Kingdom and causes the loss of over 90 million working days per annum, prevention will be cheaper than cure.

6. A VICTIM'S TALE OF STRESS

6. A VICTIM'S TALE OF STRESS

Claire Wilson

"Now I don't want you to worry but...."

My experience

Stress is a great eroder of self worth. I found this to my cost.

I am a journalist, and I am writing this because although it is stressful—even painful—to think about my experiences which one almost lives again in thinking about them, yet I want to show those people who are in a state of harmful stress now, that they are not alone, and that they should not allow themselves to have their self confidence gradually leeched away. They should try to keep hold of their self esteem, and seek help early.

For the bullies—my story is there to show you what you can do to a person and how you can destroy someone.

For those who help family, friends or a colleague who is suffering, this is a story of hope. If you try, you can help—but you may have to be patient.

Here is the story of what stress did to me.

In my case I had worked for the same organisation, a prestigious trade association, for some 18 years. For the first few years I had produced various newsletters. Probably it would have made sense to have planned my career better, but it was a comfortable job and the majority of the time I was thought of highly, and this, and a mixture of vanity, pride in my work and familiarity made me stay. I also thought that I was doing something useful, and could help large numbers of business people. I could also meet many interesting, successful and even powerful people on their own terms. The emphasis of the newsletters was on what the trade association members wanted, and indeed needed in terms of information, and I thought that I did a good job. I worked hard, and I enjoyed it. Of course I was put under some stress: I had deadlines to meet, and I was always under pressures at work—but these did not worry me. Deadlines were there to provide the adrenalin—and the end product produced its own reward.

The poison chalice came when as a journalist I was offered the job of editing the association's magazine. At first I was delighted to be offered the newly launched magazine. Unlike the newsletters, the magazine was intended to be a prestige vehicle which would come out monthly, would carry advertising, and would thereby eventually produce a healthy profit for the association.

However, the contract to sell advertising which was the key to profitability, was negotiated largely without my involvement. After a year I discovered that the "powers that be" wanted the impossible. Somehow or other they imagined that the publication would be a "cash cow" without, in the contract, giving me the power to step on the advertising agency to encourage good performance by them. I was also required to include topics which I knew would be of little relevance to the readers for purposes of company politics and self aggrandisement of certain managers. It was demanded therefore that I cut down on the information which I regarded as apposite.

For 10 years I had worked for the same highly intelligent and sensitive individual, who had to some degree supported me, but who was then himself the victim of a "palace coup" and made redundant—incidentally to the surprise of and regret of most people who knew him. Over the next five years I had no fewer than five different managers, each of whom were "the first 100 days men"—i.e. they made changes for the sake of change and in order to make their mark. A frenzied activity which made one remember the fate of cats in the Middle Ages: the only cats which were kept during the famous famine were the ones which made the most noise when bringing in the mice.

It was unfortunate for me that in my view each of these managers seemed to have bouts of irrationality (and possibly a lack of respect?) which I found hard to take. For example in one case I had organised a trip to a Latin American country to research and thereby enable me to write what I judged would be articles for the magazine useful to members. I then postponed the trip because of concerns that it would be a financial cost to the association when times were hard. However at the last minute I was able to swing a "freebie" hotel and air fare from an airline. I was then criticised for doing things at the last minute. Unjust, it seemed to me, after all the effort I had put in. This was not an isolated incident. It was a case of frequent drops of water on the soft stone of my self confidence. I started to feel less able in my job. Any small errors in text, whether or not my fault, would be pounced on, rather than help given to provide back-ups to check text, and no notice was taken of the fact that I was doing a job with half a full-time assistant which in most organisations would be allocated many more staff.

The outcome? I began drinking heavily in a local City wine bar. I never exceeded one hour for lunch, but I needed the camaraderie of what are known as SKABS (South Korea and Allied Bucket Shops) personnel. These are bankers in their 50s put into Third World Banks by the Bank of England to ensure that these establishments conduct their business properly. As such they are virtually un-sackable, and three-hour lunch-times are the norm. They provided much needed light relief for me.

A further factor which sounds insignificant, but was not, was that I was a heavy smoker, and the association moved to a smoke-free building. Suddenly I had to reduce this addiction—probably in itself a good thing, but which provided a further incentive to my going to the wine bar.

The contract for selling advertising space on the magazine was shifted by my last manager to another company on even more unfavourable terms, despite my warnings, and the principal sales person there too under-performed significantly. Despite the fact that the new contract still had no teeth, I was consistently blamed for the lack of revenue, and subjected to constant threats about the future of the magazine, although there was no effective action that I could take, as I was powerless, but carried the responsibility nevertheless. I knew that the prognosis for the magazine was not good, and this made me even more anxious, as my future seemed inextricably linked to the magazine.

The drinking continued at a greater level: not just at lunch-times now, but also in the evenings, and I progressed from wine to spirits. And my self-esteem continued to plummet.

Eventually in October 1994 the magazine was folded. I had been warned that this might happen, and was expecting it for months, but it was only when an advertiser rang me that I learned that the magazine had been suspended indefinitely. Quite a shock, and an insult to have to find out in this way—I was the editor after all. None of this was conducive to restoring my self esteem. They obviously didn't rate me high enough to tell me first—so I thought in my now thoroughly stressed, muddle-headed and debilitated state. I did not put this lack of communication down, as I should have done, to rank bad management, and a mixture of cowardice and cruelty on the part of my manager.

I now knew that the magazine was gone indefinitely, but still I was given no indication as to what my fate would be. Would or wouldn't I be made redundant? What was I facing? Would I be taken into another department? What would happen to my assistant? I felt some responsibility for her too. I was by now well over 40 years old, and had to face the extra difficulties of ageism—not so easy to find, or for me in my low self esteem, even to look for a new job. I regarded many of my work colleagues as part of my life, which had tended to revolve around my job and workplace. I did not want to lose them. Quite a load of pressures, compounded by my pride, which would not let me unburden too much to others.

I spent two awful months shuffling paper, and trying to be of use to the organisation, with no specific role given to me, other than to produce a specification on alternatives to publishing the magazine in-house. This too was hard, since effectively my research was aimed at writing myself out of a job.

During this time, I continued to drink to excess. Additionally I let my appearance deteriorate. My shoes were scuffed. I did not visit the hairdresser, and I started to drink before going to work. My appetite diminished and I lost a lot of weight. The alcohol obviously compounded problems since, although I believe I never appeared drunk, it put a strain on my finances. I also developed irritable bowel syndrome, and frequently vomited before going to work, and also occasionally during the day.

I was then particularly unfortunate in my manager, who while he appeared mild to those who did not know him, was in fact a selective bully, and seemed to take a positive delight in my downward spiral. I was needled, and felt it. As Jean Paul Sartre wrote "Hell is other people". I was not alone in finding him an inadequate manager. During the two years he was in office he managed a team of eight, and managed to lose six staff, and another nearly left. It is no excuse for him that I believe that he himself felt threatened generally and possibly specifically by my knowledge and experience; and maybe felt better when he watched and needled me. It was left to the Chief Executive in early January 1995 to tell me that my job was "at risk", his euphemism to say that I was on my way out.

When the "chop" did come, my manager announced the day before that he wanted a meeting, and, when asked, refused to say what the topic would be. I passed a very troublesome 24 hours. In the end the personnel manager indicated that they "were not proud" about the way in which I had been treated. The interview took place at noon, and after 18 years I had two weeks' notice. I asked to go home. I headed for the wine bar, got "blotto", and went back to my house.

This was a Thursday, and the next day I felt very agitated, and didn't feel up to going to the office. I lacked the motivation even to go in and do a tidying-up exercise. I did not want to see my work colleagues, and see the compassion in their eyes, or the triumph in the face of my manager, who by now I actively hated. A strong word for a very destructive and exhausting emotion.

Some 12 years previously I had experienced a violent burglary, during which I had been badly beaten up, and had contracted agoraphobia as a result. There was a difference, however, in that then I had felt valued in my job, and despite the unpleasantness of having a face that looked as though I had been in a car crash (according to one colleague), and the difficulties caused by the neurosis, I struggled to work every day.

Now the experience of being de-hired and the stress of the previous months accumulated, and brought back the old agoraphobia with a vengeance. I was terrified of going out. Additionally, never the tidiest of people, I let the house and housework slip badly. I fabricated all sorts of excuses not to go into the office during the period they were allowing me to use the premises as a base to search for another job—I was unwell—I had a bad back etc ... In fact I was, of course, deeply depressed.

Eventually I rang a former colleague, who was shocked by my general state, appearance and weight loss. She rang my GP who had me admitted on a voluntary basis into a psychiatric ward, where I stayed for five days. This is when one learns who one's allies are. I was visited by various friends, mostly work colleagues.

Something positive has to be taken out of every experience. My stay in a psychiatric ward was valuable. The people in the ward in which I had been placed were those with mild forms of neuroses and psychoses, predominantly in their early 20s. A number were anorexics. The fact that they were so young, and hopefully getting better, was helpful to me, as many seemed to be on their way to half-way homes—a moral judgement on society being that, for the most part, had they had decent home backgrounds most would not have been there in the first place.

I was being put together again. Being "dried out" did not cause me great difficulty. I was so weak from not eating that I couldn't stand unaided, and felt immeasurably better when I came out—even if I did still look gaunt. At least I had been able to wheel the anorexics backwards and forwards from the telephone booth (they were not allowed to go out of their rooms unless in wheelchairs).

Once I was out and home again, one work colleague and friend who also lived not far from me, took me by the scruff of the neck, and made me have my house renovated, and encouraged me to embark as soon as possible on a career of freelance journalism. Without the support of my friends, I do not think that I would have survived, or indeed have mustered the energy to survive. Redundancy and *ex gratia* payments were gradually settled which gave me a few weeks' grace, but no cushion as such, and I started the long haul back to normality.

I can't pretend it was easy to come to terms with the need to put myself together. I suddenly saw that both I and the house were wrecks and needed total re-furbishment. I started the rounds of dentist and hairdresser and just a few clothes shops—for finances were low, and had to be carefully marshalled. A sympathetic builder dealt with the house, and helped me too by his kindly presence, and by making my home charming to live in once more, so I would have a cheerful environment.

What happened then?

My financial position in respect of state monetary benefits was difficult, in that as I had been paid a sum in lieu of notice, I was only entitled to have my National Insurance Contribution payments paid for the notice period—in my case three months. I therefore had to do something about income.

The hazards of self-employment

Initially the freedom of self-employment was great. I could capitalise on my old contacts. There was the cushion of redundancy money—but that quickly ran out. Others that I had encountered in self-employment were delighted to be out of the "wage slave" stranglehold, but it is not to everyone's ability, and can, for that reason, be stressful.

I quickly discovered that idiosyncrasies, tolerated in a corporate world, were not in the remit of the freelance. Gone were the one-hour lunch-breaks. Gone was the option that if you had a cold then you could phone in saying that you were poorly. If you do that, you simply do not get paid. And you have to be more subservient than perhaps you were used to when you had a senior position in the corporate hierarchy. Dress code is important, as many officials made redundant from Government departments find out. Forgetting about ponytails (for men) is just one instance.

Perks are OFF!

Suddenly, off the agenda are the perks of full-time employment. No more interest-free travel ticket loans. This means that you have to plan your journeys very carefully to cram as many meetings as possible into one day in the same area. The best option in London is the one-day travel card at roughly half the cost of travelling during the morning rush hour. However, as this only allows you to travel after 9.30 am, its use is dependent on making arrangements to arrive later at your destination.

Other perks which vanish include small things such as luncheon vouchers which make an unexpected difference to your budget. There is the use of office stationery, pens, envelopes and other bits and bobs all of which add up to a tidy sum. The advantages of not having to worry about the telephone bill or the cost of faxes sent while in the office are not to be sniffed at. Over and above all for some, there is corporate entertainment, which can save on home food bills, albeit add to the waistline. Gas and electricity bills can no longer be handled by standing order because of the irregularity of monthly income.

Oh the paperwork!

Then there is the personal taxation paperwork. No longer is there a company accounts department to sort out your PAYE. Instead, I soon learned that it is essential to keep full records and every receipt relating to business and other expenses, whether for council tax, computer cartridges, stamps, stationery, telephone bills or whatever. Even if these are kept in a shoe box, it is still worthwhile to retain them. Unless you are a financial whizz, get yourself an accountant. He or she will be able to advise, at a price, what you can claim in terms of overheads such as heating, lighting, telephone and fax bills. But again, these records need to be kept in an organised way, and you have to turn yourself into an administrator and filer of documents, however that may go against your creative talents. You won't be able to ignore all these details—indeed if you do your liability could quickly escalate— and every minute of your accountant's time saved saves you fees.

Assessing proper fees to ask, and then collecting them, is, I find, often difficult and embarrassing. People may be happy to ask me to do work for them, but less happy to pay. This obviously affects my cash flow, and adds pressures, but is, apparently, a problem encountered by every freelance person.

Financial extras

Back on the financial front, there is the question of pensions. The issue of converting your corporate pension into a personal pension is not without its hazards, given the number of "cowboys" still in the field, and there are many tied agents who still operate to their own, rather than your advantage, despite tighter regulation. If you don't quite understand a point they make, don't be afraid to ask for a clearer, preferably written explanation.

Health or sickness insurance is another important consideration. The company's private health policies give many people a comfort blanket. Now you will have to make your own provisions, at a startlingly high cost—but remember you may be able to build on the record you have already built up with the organisation which previously covered you when you were an employee.

Social aspects

On a psychological note, there is the isolation of self-employment. Possibly one of the worst things I have had to come to terms with has been the loneliness of working at home. As a single person who likes people, working at home has been hard, and the temptation is always to telephone people during the day, when tariffs are high. I discovered my telephone bills were astronomical. There was also the depression, and the temptation to drink again ... Time-wasting activities take over—I found myself watching daytime TV instead of working, and then having to slave to meet deadlines; and I would put off the telephone call I really needed to make in order to talk to a friendly voice.

The ability to talk through problems with your colleagues should not be under-estimated.

Communication leads to new ideas and stimulates creativity, so the isolation element of self-employment should not be forgotten.

For those with partners or family at home, the problems caused by getting under each other's feet is another difficulty for home-workers.

Everyone likes the security of knowing their own position, and recently redundant, even if self-employed, people can feel the lack of status. While previously you were "Joe Bloggs, Marketing Director of XYZ Plc", now you feel you are a nobody trying to make a crust. Those who have not gone through the mill themselves can be very unsympathetic—until it happens to them, which, given the trends in the USA, would appear to be becoming more likely.

The future

In the new scenario, the situation will not be as bleak as I have painted, as there will be increasing numbers of self-employed people, who will be more readily employed on short term contracts, and so they will not feel so isolated. In order not to become too stressed if this is your position, you have to just accept the new world of less secure work. Where accountants and fearful geriontocrats (i.e. old people who rule) are in a position of power, relatively highly paid, experienced but middle-aged professionals and other employees will inevitably get the chop for a variety of reasons. Those which come from accountants are based on short-termism and cost-cutting. Elsewhere, the unsaid reasons from the great and the good will include a preference for the young and malleable disinclined or unable to tell the emperor that he wears no clothes. Either way, you, as one of the new self-employed, should not be discouraged.

What should you do?

First to break out of the trap of isolation, you should try networking. There are local Chambers of Commerce, and Training and Enterprise Councils (TECs), albeit these may vary in quality depending on where you are located. They will be keen to get you to join, but it may be sensible to hold back until you have attended at least one of their events, just to assess the calibre of networking opportunities. For the male fraternity, there are the Freemasons, who are a useful source of helpful contacts for their members: and there are other organisations too.

If you decide that working at home is not for you, then there are a growing number of business centres or incubator units, some of which are run by enterprise agencies. Obviously these put up your costs, but the advantage is that you are then in the company of other people in similar situations, and with the same stresses and strains.

Conclusion

Gradually one gets used to a different pattern of work, but I still have the constant worries of all self-employed people, primarily about income. Will I earn enough to pay the mortgage and cover my expenses this month? One is only as good as one's last piece of work for a particular customer. Research is more difficult as an individual without the weight, help and facilities of an organisation behind one.

I have not kicked the problems of suffering from harmful stress. I still have good days, and bad ones. I still have to throw off the memories and the hurt, or at least try to balance them with the kindnesses of so many people. Even now I sometimes wake up in a cold sweat in the middle of the night. Stress is still there to be faced, but now it is of a different type. Everyone has a degree of harmful stress in their lives, and I am learning to cope with it. At least now I feel I am master of my own destiny.

Self-employment in my view is hard, but is still better than working in a situation of counter-productive office politics, bullying, and other invidious stresses.

I think that I will hack it, and I hope that you will too.

Appendix 1. EXAMPLE OF AN OCCUPATIONAL HEALTH POLICY

Employee well-being in the Post Office

Health is a state of complete physical, psychological and social well-being. The Post Office Mission statement is supported by values that include caring for fellow employees. The Health & Safety policy of the Post Office confirms the commitment to achieving the highest standards of health.

The well-being of staff is essential to achieving a high quality business.

Employee Support and Occupational Health Services work with Post Office managers in maintaining and improving the well-being of Post Office employees. This enables line managers to meet statutory duties under health and safety legislation, assess and reduce risks to employee health, and to promote a healthy, efficient workforce.

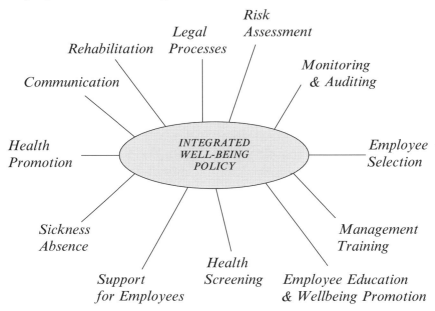

It is a statutory duty of all managers to ensure that risks to health, safety or welfare at work are identified, eliminated or reduced and that staff have adequate information and training.

An integrated Wellness Policy is the Post Office approach for ensuring that all aspects of employee well-being are considered. Professional support in achieving this requires a co-ordinated approach complemented by expert staff in Employee Support and Occupational Health services.

In this way we support the Post Office Health and Safety policy to initiate and monitor the effectiveness of Health and Safety policy.

Appendix 2. USEFUL ADDRESSES

HMSO Books
Publications Centre
PO Box 276
LONDON
SW8 5DT
Tel: 0171 873 0011/0022 (24 hrs)

Trade Counters and Bookshops
49 High Holborn
LONDON
WC1V 6HB
Tel: 0171 873 0011

9-21 Princess Street
MANCHESTER
M60 8AS
Tel: 0161 834 7201

Southey House
33 Wine Street
BRISTOL
BS1 2BQ
Tel: 0117 9264306

16 Arthur Street
BELFAST
BT1 4GD
Tel: 01232 238451

258 Broad Street
BIRMINGHAM
B1 2HE
Tel: 0121 643 3740

71 Lothian Road
EDINBURGH
EH3 9AZ
Tel: 0131 228 4181

British Association for Counselling
BAC
37a Sheep Street
RUGBY
Warwickshire
CU21 3BX
Tel: 01788 578328
Fax: 01788 562189

Commission of the European Communities
Rue de la Loi 200
B-1049 Brussels
Belgium
Tel: (322) 299 111
Fax: 0171 973 1900 (London office)

The British Register of Complementary Practitioners
PO Box 194
LONDON
SE16 1QL
Tel: 0171 237 5175

Employee Assistance & Professionals Association
EAPA
Wyvals Court
Swallowfield
READING
Berks
RG7 1PY

European Foundation for the Improvement of Living and Working Conditions
Loughlinstown House
Shankill
County Dublin
Republic of Ireland
Tel: (3531) 282 6888
Fax: (3531) 282 6456

Health Education Authority
Hamilton House
Mabeldon Place
LONDON
WC1H 9TX
Tel: 0171 383 3833
Fax: 0171 387 0550

Industrial Society
Principal Office
Peter Runge House
3 Carlton House Terrace
LONDON
SW1Y 5DG
Tel: 0171 839 4300
Fax: 0171 839 3898

Institute of Personnel & Development
IPD House
Camp Road
LONDON
SW19 4UX
Tel: 0181 971 9000
Fax: 0181 263 3333

NFER Nelson (Occupational Stress Indicator)
ASE Division
Darville House
2 Oxford Road East
WINDSOR
Berkshire
SL4 1DE

On-Site Massage Association
c/o D Woodhouse
New Street
Charfield
WOTTON-UNDER-EDGE
Glos
GL12 8TS
Tel: 01453 521530
Fax: 01453 521530

Sports Council
16 Upper Woburn Place
LONDON
WC1 0QP
Tel: 0171 388 1277
Fax: 0171 388 7048

Stress Management Systems
Performance Support International
6-16 Huntsworth Mews
LONDON
NW1 6DD
Tel: 0171 724 8599

References

BAGLIONI, A.J. Jr., COOPER, C.L. and HINGLEY, P. (1990). "Job stress, mental health and job satisfaction among UK senior nurses", *Stress Medicine*, 6, 9–20.

BERRIDGE, J., COOPER, C.L. and HIGHLEY, C. (1991). *EAPs and Workplace Counselling* (Chichester: John Wiley & Sons).

CARTWRIGHT, S., and COOPER, C.L. (1992). *Mergers and Acquisitions: The Human Factor* (Oxford: Butterworth Heinemann).

CARTWRIGHT, S., COOPER, C.L. and BARRON, A. (1993). "An investigation of the relationship between occupational stress and accidents amongst company car drivers", *Journal of General Management*, 19(2), 78–85.

COOPER, C.L. (1996). "Hot under the Collar", *Times Higher Education Supplement*, June 21, p. 15.

COOPER, C.L. and CARTWRIGHT, S. (1996). *Mental Health and Stress in the Workplace* (London: HMSO).

COOPER, C.L., DAVIDSON, M.J. and ROBINSON, P. (1982). "Stress in the police service", *Journal of Occupational Medicine*, 24, (1), 30–6.

COOPER, C.L., MALLINGER, M. and KAHN, R. (1978). "Identifying sources of occupational stress amongst dentists", *Journal of Occupational Psychology*, 51, 227–34.

COOPER, C.L., SLOAN, S.J. and WILLIAMS, S. (1988). *Occupational Stress Indicator Management Guide* (Windsor: NFER Nelson).

COOPER, C.L. and LEWIS, G. (1993). *The Workplace Revolution: Managing Today's Dual Career Families* (London: Kogan).

COOPER, C.L. and LEWIS, S. (1995). "Balancing the home:work interface: A European perspective" *Human Resource Management Review*, 5(4), 289–305.

COOPER, C.L. and SMITH, M.J. (1985). *Job Stress and Blue Collar Work* (Chichester and New York: John Wiley & Sons).

COOPER, C.L. and WILLIAMS, S. (1994). *Creating Healthy Work Organizations* (Chichester: John Wiley & Sons).

DAVIDSON, M.J. and COOPER, C.L. (1992). *Shattering the Glass Ceiling: The Woman Manager* (London: Paul Chapman Publishing).

EARNSHAW, J. and COOPER, C.L. (1996). *Stress and Employer Liability* (London: IPD Books).

EDWARDS, J.R. and COOPER, C.L. (1990). "The person-environment fit approach to stress: Recurring problems and some suggested solutions", *Journal of Organizational Behaviour*, 11, 293–307.

FRENCH, J.R.P. and CAPLAN, R.D. (1970). "Organizational stress and individual strain" in Marlow, A. (ed.) *The Failure of Success*.

IVANCEVICH, J.M. and MATTESON, M.T. (1980). *Stress and Work* (Illinois: Scott Foresman & Co).

KAHN, H. and COOPER, C.L. (1986). "Computing stress", *Current Psychological Research and Reviews*, Summer, 148–62.

KARASEK, R. and THEORELL, T. (1990). *Healthy Work: Stress Productivity and the Reconstruction of Working Life* (New York: John Wiley & Sons).

SKOV, D., VALBJORN, O. and PEDERSON, B.V. (1990). "Influence of indoor climate on the sick building syndrome in an office environment", *Scandinavian Journal of Work Environment and Health*, 16, (5), 363–71.

WALLACE, H., LEVANS, M. and SLINGER, G. (1988). "Blue collar stress" in Cooper, C.L. and Payne, R. (eds.) *Causes, Coping and Consequences of Stress at Work* (Chichester: John Wiley & Sons).

Index